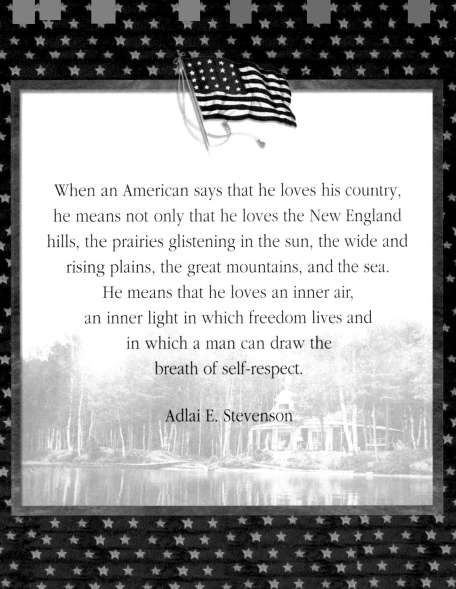

When an American says that he loves his country,
he means not only that he loves the New England
hills, the prairies glistening in the sun, the wide and
rising plains, the great mountains, and the sea.
He means that he loves an inner air,
an inner light in which freedom lives and
in which a man can draw the
breath of self-respect.

Adlai E. Stevenson

1,001
REASONS *to* LOVE™
AMERICA

HUBERT PEDROLI & MARY TIEGREEN

Stewart, Tabori & Chang
New York

Published in 2004 by
Stewart, Tabori & Chang
115 West 18th Street
New York, NY 10011

Canadian Distribution:
Canadian Manda Group
One Atlantic Avenue, Suite 105
Toronto, Ontario, M6K 3E7
Canada

Library of Congress Cataloging-in-Publication Data
Pedroli, Hubert.
1,001 reasons to love America/ Hubert Pedroli & Mary Tiegreen-1st ed.
p. cm.
ISBN 1-58479-377-5 (hardcover)
1. National characteristics, American-Miscellanea. 2. United states-Civilization-Miscellanea. 3. Popular culture-United States-Miscellanea.
4. United States-Description and travel-Miscellanea. . I. Title: One thousand and one reasons to love America. II. Tiegreen, Mary. III. Title.
E169.1.P39 2004
973-dc22
2004006997

1,001 Reasons to Love America is a book in the 1,001 REASONS TO LOVE™ Series.

1,001 REASONS TO LOVE™ is a trademark of Mary Tiegreen and Hubert Pedroli.

Printed in China

10 9 8 7 6 5 4 3 2 1

First Printing

Stewart, Tabori & Chang is a subsidiary of

LA MARTINIÈRE
GROUPE

CONTENTS

Introduction

Creating a list of 1,001 things to love about America seemed an impossible task at the beginning. There are 1,001 things to love about summer evenings and Sunday mornings alone. 1,001 things to love about the spectacular Pacific coastline or the Rocky Mountains or an Arizona sunset, and well over 700 things to love about the movie *It's a Wonderful Life.* Our history and heritage represents in excess of 10,000 things of which to be proud. And the reasons to love freedom are far beyond our ability to count.

We love the taste of New England clam chowder and Oreo cookies, and the smell of popcorn at the movies on a Saturday afternoon. The familiar sounds of American life: the bell ringing on the Good Humor truck, or the cheer from the bleachers after a home run. And we love at least 50 things about the 1955 Thunderbird convertible.

There are over 1,200,000 things to love about American music. Tastes may vary and styles come and go, but who doesn't love B.B. King singing "The Thrill is Gone," or Willie Nelson doing "Always on My Mind"? And then there is Gershwin and Ellington and The Beach Boys and Elvis! And what about all the amazing things that were discovered or invented here in America? What would the world be like without safety pins, post-it notes, the Heimlich Maneuver, or the Frisbee?

The incredible landscape of America offers well over 3,000,000 places to visit and things to love. We are blessed with the wonder and wilderness of our National Parks, hundreds of scenic byways, and 10,000 places to hike and camp and drive and be alone in nature. We can sleep in a Wigwam and visit The Shoe House, or marvel at the world's largest catsup bottle.

There are countless American heroes, both well-known and everyday people, who give us a reason to be proud. There are pioneers and presidents and landmarks and legends. The right to vote, free elections, and the ability to have a voice in our government. Sometimes we take these things for granted, but it is not this way everywhere in the world.

The list is endless, and yet we had to reduce it down to 1,001. Our hope is that this book serves as an inspiration to discover other things to love about our great country.

Hubert Pedroli & Mary Tiegreen

Land of the Free

Ever since 1776, Americans have been
protecting and defending their freedom.
Great speeches have rekindled liberty's
flame when the nation was in danger, and
great military, economic and social battles
have been fought in liberty's name.

Fundamentally, however, it is in the daily
actions of ordinary Americans that freedom
finds its most reliable defense.

The human heart yearns for peace and
love and freedom. Peace heals, elevates,
and invigorates the spirit.

Michael DeBakey

1
Freedom

Our freedom is a priceless gift.
It gives us the opportunity to achieve our
highest potential and create great things.
It is a beacon of hope for a better future
for ourselves and our children. It gives life to the
idea that all things are possible.

THE SURVIVAL AND THE SUCCESS OF LIBERTY

Let the word go forth from this time and place, to friend and foe alike, that the torch has been passed to a new generation of Americans—born in this century, tempered by war, disciplined by a hard and bitter peace, proud of our ancient heritage—and unwilling to witness or permit the slow undoing of those human rights to which this Nation has always been committed, and to which we are committed today at home and around the world.

Let every nation know, whether it wishes us well or ill, that we shall pay any price, bear any burden, meet any hardship, support any friend, oppose any foe, in order to assure the survival and the success of liberty.

John F. Kennedy's inaugural address, January 20, 1961

2
A willingness to sacrifice to
protect and defend liberty

Five things we should never take for granted

3
The right to vote
Americans have the opportunity to choose their government and to change it, through free elections. Each vote counts!

4
Freedom of speech
The Constitution protects our right to express our ideas and opinions freely, in speech and in writing.

5
Freedom to assemble
Americans are free to gather peacefully in groups, and to protest government policies.

6
Freedom of religion
The right to worship as we choose, or not at all, is guaranteed by the Constitution of the United States.

7
Strength in our diversity
This land of opportunity has welcomed countless groups that all add to the rich mix of American culture.

CONTINUED PEACE & PROSPERITY
PRESIDENT AL GORE
VICE PRESIDENT JOE LIEBERMAN

HARRY S. TRUMAN

McCARTHY 76

WALLACE '48

JIMMY CARTER FOR PRESIDENT

KENNEDY and JOHNSON

8
Campaigns, polls,
primaries and caucuses,
national conventions,
and free elections

EVOTE

~ 16 ~

MILESTONES

TURNING POINTS IN AMERICA'S HISTORY

The history of America shines with acts of courage and vision, each
building upon the principles of freedom and fairness upon which
our country was founded.

9
The Boston Tea Party

The Boston Tea Party was a
protest against tax policies
imposed by the British.

The colonists saw the "Tea
Act" as the beginning of
British control over Colonial
business. In protest, "The Sons
of Liberty," dressed as Mohawk
warriors, boarded three British ships in
Boston Harbor and dumped 342 chests of
tea into the sea on December 16, 1773.

Of this bold action, John
Adams wrote, "There is a
dignity, a majesty, a
sublimity, in this last effort
of the patriots that I
greatly admire."

10
The Writing of the Declaration of Independence

In the spring of 1776, Americans had been at war for a year. In June, the Continental Congress named a committee of five to draft a declaration of independence. The committee chose Thomas Jefferson to write the draft. Jefferson drew upon ideas of great political thinkers including England's John Locke who wrote in 1688 that government is a contract, or compact, between the government and the people. If the government did not live up to that contract, the people had the right to change the government or create a new one.

Jefferson's draft of the Declaration of Independence was a bold statement of a people's right to create their own government. The men who signed the document knew they were risking everything, but they willingly added their names. After numerous drafts and much debate, the Continental Congress approved the Declaration of Independence on July 4, 1776.

11
Surrender of the British at Yorktown

After Washington led the Continental army to victory in the North, the British army was finally trapped in the South on the coast of Virginia at Yorktown. Washington led his Continental army and a 5,000-man French force on a 500-mile march from New York, past Philadelphia, and finally to Yorktown in late September. Washingon's army surrounded the British by land while the French fleet, anchored off the coast, blocked them at sea. After a three-week battle, Cornwallis surrendered on October 19, 1781. Americans had won their independence.

We the People

of the U...

insure domestic Tranquility, provide for the common defence, pr...
and our Posterity, do ordain and establish this Constitution for th...

Article. 1

Section. 1. All legislative Powers herein granted shall be vested...
of Representatives.

Section. 2. The House of Representatives shall be composed of M...
in each State shall have the Qualifications requisite for Electors of the most nu...

No Person shall be a Representative who shall not have attain...
and who shall not, when elected, be an Inhabitant of that State in which h...

Representatives and direct Taxes shall be apportioned among the s...
Numbers, which shall be determined by adding to the whole Number of fre...
not taxed, three fifths of all other Persons. The actual Enumeration sha...
and within every subsequent Term of ten Years, in such Manner as they...
thirty Thousand, but each State shall have at Least one Representative...
entitled to chuse three, Massachusetts eight, Rhode-Island and Provi...
eight, Delaware one, Maryland six, Virginia ten, North Carolina fiv...

When vacancies happen in the Representation from any State...

The House of Representatives shall chuse their Speaker and oth...

Section. 3. The Senate of the United States shall be composed of two...

12
The negotiation of the Constitution in Philadelphia

In 1787, fifty-five delegates from thirteen states met in Philadelphia to create the U.S. Constitution which would establish the nation's democratic structure. When they were done, they had created one of history's great documents – a framework that has served the nation for more than two centuries and has been a model for other governments around the world.

Beginning in autumn of 1787, state conventions met to ratify the Constitution. Nine of the thirteen states had to approve before the Constitution could go into effect. There was vigorous debate, because many people feared that the new government would have too much power. In Massachusetts, for example, ratification succeeded only after delegates promised they would add a bill of rights – the first ten amendments to the Constitution.

The final victory for ratification, in late June 1788, was very close. By the spring of 1790, all thirteen states had approved the constitution.

When the new congress met in 1789, James Madison proposed several amendments to the Constitution, as the Federalists had promised at some state conventions. Congress approved the proposal, and the first ten amendments to the Constitution were called the Bill of Rights.

The first four amendments list the individual rights of Americans, such as freedom of speech, freedom of the press, and freedom of religion. The next four are protections of people who are arrested, including the right to a speedy trial. The ninth amendment states that other rights of the people are also protected even though they are not listed, and the tenth says that powers not given to the government belong to the states or to the people.

INDEPENDENCE HALL
AND
LIBERTY BELL.

Lincoln's Gettysburg Address

On November 19, 1863, Lincoln delivered his famous speech at Gettysburg, in which he sought a basis for peace and reconciliation. The Gettysburg Address was an eloquent statement of the meaning of the war and a reaffirmation of America's great experiment in democracy. It was a short speech written on White House stationery during the train ride to Gettysburg, Pennsylvania, and delivered at the dedication of the Gettysburg battlefield cemetery where a fierce battle had been fought in July 1863 between the North and the South.

FOUR SCORE AND SEVEN YEARS AGO our fathers brought forth, upon this continent, a new nation, conceived in liberty, and dedicated to the proposition that "all men are created equal."

Now we are engaged in a great civil war, testing whether that nation, or any nation so conceived, and so dedicated, can long endure. We are met on a great battle field of that war. We have come to dedicate a portion of it, as a final resting place for those who died here, that the nation might live. This we may, in all propriety do. But, in a larger sense, we can not dedicate—we can not consecrate—we can not hallow, this ground—The brave men, living and dead, who struggled here, have hallowed it, far above our poor power to add or detract. The world will little note, nor long remember what we say here; but it can never forget what they did here.

It is rather for us, the living, we here be dedicated to the great task remaining before us—that, from these honored dead we take increased devotion to that cause for which they here, gave the last full measure of devotion—that we here highly resolve these dead shall not have died in vain; that this nation, shall have a new birth of freedom, and that government of the people, by the people, for the people, shall not perish from the earth.

14 Lincoln's Emancipation Proclamation

President Lincoln's concern was the preservation of the Union; he wanted to bring the southern states back into the Union. In September 1862, when his offer of compromise failed to accomplish this, he carried out the threat he had made and on January 1, 1863, issued his declaration freeing the slaves.

15 Wilson's Fourteen Points

Before the end of World War I in November 1918, President Woodrow Wilson presented his plan to create a lasting peace after the war. He called it the Fourteen Points, believing it was part of America's special mission to "aid in the establishment of a just democracy throughout the world." Issues raised in the Fourteen Points, such as seeking justice in international relations, allowing the "self-determination of people," creating alliances, and the quest for peace, have continued in importance for nearly a century.

16 The women's suffrage movement

The drive for women's voting rights, or women's suffrage, gained momentum in the early 1900's. African-American men had been given the right to vote in 1870 with the passage of the Fifteenth Amendment to the Constitution. But at the turn of the century, women of all races were still denied that right. By 1913, twelve states had granted voting rights to women, but Congress held back from passing an amendment to the Constitution.

During World War I (1917-1920), huge numbers of jobs became available because so many men were in the armed services. Women began to work at jobs they had not held before—delivering mail and driving trolleys and ambulances, for example. President Woodrow Wilson said women's suffrage was "vital to winning the war."

By 1920 the women's suffrage movement was victorious with the passage of the Nineteenth Amendment of the Constitution, which gave women the right to vote in all elections at the local, state, and national levels of government.

17 The New Deal

In October 1929, the stock market collapsed. More than 86,000 businesses failed including many banks. People lost their life savings, and wages for people still employed were cut by 60%. Franklin Delano Roosevelt was sworn in as president on March 4, 1933, and in his first hundred days launched the New Deal, a series of legislative proposals that promised dramatic changes. Some of the most important acts of the New Deal years included the Social Security Act, the creation of the National Labor Relations Board (NLRB), and the establishment of the Works Progress Administration (WPA). New Deal programs fell into three categories: relief programs aimed at reducing suffering; recovery programs to revive business and agriculture; and reform programs to correct problems that had contributed to the Depression.

Posters created by WPA artists.

18 The Four Freedoms

Before America officially entered World War II in December 1941, President Franklin Delano Roosevelt and Britain's Prime Minister Winston Churchill met on a warship off the coast of Newfoundland for talks. They agreed on the Atlantic Charter, a statement saying that the Allied nations were not interested in taking any territory, but rather in restoring peace. The Charter included Roosevelt's idea of the "Four Freedoms": freedom of speech and religion, and freedom from fear and want.

> "The United Nations is our one great hope for a peaceful and free world."
>
> Ralph Bunche

19 The creation of the United Nations

Although World War II did not end until 1945, in November 1943, the United States and the Allies recognized the need to establish an organization dedicated to international peace and security. Two weeks after President Roosevelt's death in April 1945, the United Nations organization was founded. Eight hundred delegates from 50 nations met in San Francisco and produced the United Nations Charter, which was approved 89 to 2 by the U.S. Senate.

20 The campaign for civil liberties

From 1960 to 1969, inspiring leaders such as Martin Luther King, Jr. fought racial prejudice with non-violent demonstrations and legislative change, culminating in the Civil Rights Act of 1964.

The non-violent effort for social justice began in earnest in 1955 with the Montgomery, Alabama, bus boycott led by Dr. King. It lasted a year, and in 1956 the Supreme Court ruled that segregated buses were unconstitutional.

On June 11, 1963, President John F. Kennedy announced he was sending a bill to Congress that would make discrimination on the basis of race illegal. On August 28, 1963, the "March on Washington for Jobs and Freedom" drew more than 200,000 people in support of the bill. There, Dr. King delivered his famous speech: "I have a dream…"

By 1964 President Lyndon Johnson had pushed the Civil Rights Act through Congress. It outlawed racial discrimination in all public places. Many called the act the "second Emancipation Proclamation." It was over 100 years since President Lincoln's Emancipation Proclamation in 1863.

President Lyndon Johnson signs the The Civil Rights Act on July 2, 1964.

Landmarks, Symbols & Sacred Places

These cherished symbols and landmarks represent America's spirit, courage, creativity, potential, and love of freedom.

21
The Liberty Bell in Philadelphia

22
Monticello, Thomas Jefferson's
mountaintop home, in Charlottesville, Virginia

23
The Lincoln Memorial in Washington, D.C.

24
The Golden Gate Bridge in San Francisco

25
The Space Needle in Seattle

26
New York's Empire State Building

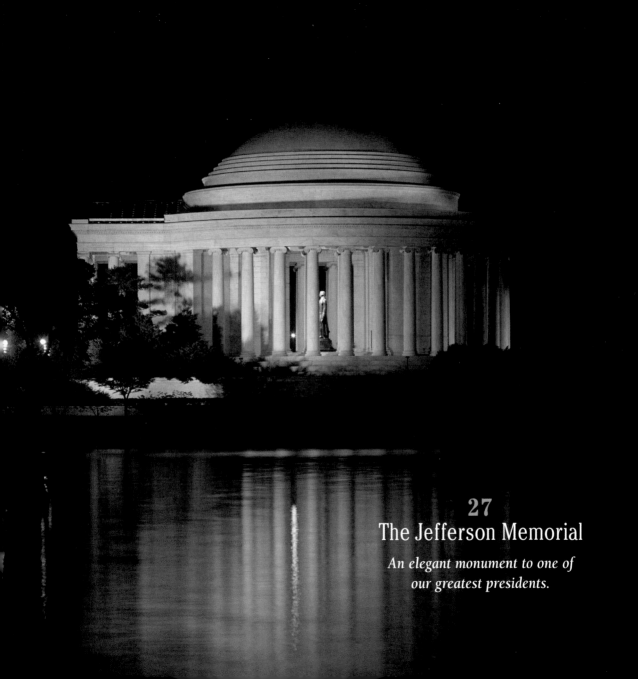

27
The Jefferson Memorial

*An elegant monument to one of
our greatest presidents.*

28
The Brooklyn Bridge

*This magnificent icon of 19th-century
American design and engineering was
begun in January of 1870 and officially
opened on May 24, 1883. Businesses in
New York and Brooklyn closed at noon
and bells rang all over town.
The fireworks began around 8:00 p.m.
More than 150,000 people crossed the
bridge on opening day, and
each paid one cent.*

29
Old Faithful Geyser,
Yellowstone National Park

30
The Kennedy Space Center,
Titusville, Florida

31
The Hoover Dam, Nevada

32
The Vietnam Veterans Memorial,
Washington, D.C.

33
The Gateway Arch, St. Louis, Missouri

This incredible structure overlooking the Mississippi River, completed in 1963, is a monument to westward expansion in America. It is 630 feet high and 630 feet wide at the base. A tram carries visitors to the viewing area at the top. Architect Eero Saarinen designed this grand arch with the hope that it would be "a monument which would have lasting significance and would be a landmark of our time."

34 The Hollywood Sign

Created in 1923 on Mt. Lee, this famous sign was maintained until 1939 by a caretaker who lived in a small cabin behind the first "L." Each letter is 50 feet tall, and the total length of the word is 450 feet. In 1973, the Hollywood sign was declared a historical cultural monument.

35 The Statue of Liberty

Welcoming visitors to America, she has been gracing New York Harbor since 1886.

36 The White House

37 Camp David

38 Graceland

39 The Alamo

40 The Continental Divide

41 The Washington Monument

A grand obelisk overlooking the National Mall. Construction began on July 4, 1848, but was halted in 1854 when the monument was 152 feet tall. Twenty years later, construction resumed and the monument was completed in December of 1884.

42
Niagara Falls

This popular destination for honeymooners lies between the two Great Lakes, Ontario and Erie.

43
Federal Hall

A bronze statue of George Washington stands on the site of the Federal Hall National Memorial. Overlooked by busy Wall Street workers, this site has tremendous historical significance. It was here that freedom of the press was established in 1735, The Stamp Act Congress was held in October of 1765, the first U.S. capital was established in 1789, the first U.S. Congress met on March 4, 1789, the U.S. federal government was formed, the first U.S. president was inaugurated on April 30, 1789, and the Bill of Rights was adopted on September 25, 1789.

44
Mt. Rushmore

In 1927, sculptor Gutzon Borglum designed his "Shrine to Democracy" with 60-foot busts of Washington, Jefferson, Lincoln, and Theodore Roosevelt (representing the birth, growth, preservation and development of America, respectively). Construction took place during the Depression and was completed by unemployed miners with help from fund-raisers.

45
The Oval Office

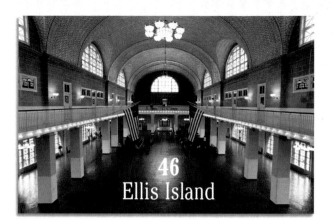

46
Ellis Island

47
The American Eagle

The Bald Eagle became America's National Emblem on June 20, 1782, at the Second Continental Congress, much to the dismay of Benjamin Franklin who preferred the turkey, "a much more respectable Bird." Today, the Eagle is a living symbol of freedom, courage, strength, power, and vision.

48
The Twin Towers of the World Trade Center

A sacred place of tragedy, sacrifice, and American courage.

THE STAR SPANGLED BANNER.

O! long may it wave,
O'er the land of the free,
And the home of the brave.

PUBLISHED BY CURRIER & IVES.

ELMHURST

FLAG DAY

JUNE 18
1939

DU PAGE COUNTY CENTENNIAL

For President
ABRAM LINCOLN.

For Vice President
HANNIBAL HAMLIN.

To the MINER

To the miner let me say that he stands where the farmer does; the work of the world waits on him. If he slacks or fails armies and statesmen are helpless. He also is enlisted in the great service army.

Woodrow Wilson

DEPARTMENT OF THE INTERIOR
Franklin K. Lane, Secretary

U.S. MARINES

MILITARY TRAINING TRAVEL

EDUCATION DEVELOPMENT

SOLDIERS OF THE SEA

49
Old Glory

The Stars and Stripes have been a powerful symbol of America for over two hundred years.

PATRIOTIC SONGS

Inspired by the beauty of the land, brave moments in battle, and love of country, these songs evoke the imagery of a proud nation and stir the heart of all Americans.

50 America the Beautiful

Once referred to as "A. the B." by its author, Katharine Lee Bates, America the Beautiful *was the marriage of Bates's poem of the same name, and the music of Samuel Ward's* Materna. *The words and music were first combined in 1904, and the song as we know it today was first published in 1910, seven years after Ward's death.*

Bates's inspiration came during a train trip to Colorado in 1893. In Chicago she saw the "alabaster" buildings of the World's Fair, passed "amber waves of grain" while traveling through Kansas, and reached the "purple mountain majesties" of the Rockies.

According to Samuel Ward, the melody for Materna *just popped into his head on the way home to Newark from Coney Island.*

51 The Star-Spangled Banner

Written by Francis Scott Key, the poem was inspired by the site of a huge 30-foot by 40-foot American flag that flew over Fort McHenry during the War of 1812.

On September 13, 1814, the fort, which defended Baltimore, had been under British bombardment for 25 hours. Finally, "at the dawn's early light," Key was able to see the flag still waving above the small, courageous fort.

Legend has it that he took an envelope from his pocket and began writing the poem that we sing today. The melody was borrowed from an old English drinking song. The Star-Spangled Banner *officially became our national anthem on March 3, 1931.*

52 America

The verse to the beloved song that begins with the words "My country 'tis of thee" was written by Samuel Francis Smith in 1832. The melody was inspired by a German song called God Bless Our Native Land, and is the same melody as Britain's anthem, God Save the Queen/King.

Some of the lines in the song have been celebrated in musicals, other songs and speeches. Of Thee I Sing, a musical by George and Ira Gershwin, lifted the spirits of audiences during the Depression.

"Let freedom ring," the last line of the first verse, was a powerful theme in Martin Luther King's speech delivered at the Lincoln Memorial in August of 1963.

53 God Bless America

Irving Berlin first composed this popular song in 1918, but put it aside. In 1938, with America on the brink of war, Berlin resurrected the song, and America first heard it on Armistice Day in 1938 when Kate Smith sang it on the radio. It enjoyed overwhelming popularity, and Berlin made an enormous amount of money from the song. In 1940, he set up the "God Bless America Fund," and royalties went to the Boy Scouts and Girl Scouts of America.

54 This Land is Your Land

Woody Guthrie wrote this song while on a cross-country hitchhiking trip in 1940. While it was written just after the Dust Bowl years and the difficult times of the Great Depression, the tune is celebratory, and the words are empowering and full of pride. The original fourth line was "God blessed America for me," a reference to Berlin's popular song.

TEN GREAT AMERICAN PRESIDENTS

Every president has faced challenges while in office, but these ten men rose to the occasion and served their country during exceptional times.

55
George Washington
(served 1789-97)

Regarded as the father of our country, Washington led the Continental Army to win America's independence from Britain in the American Revolution. His courage and wisdom won the trust of his peers, who chose him to preside over the convention that drafted the United States Constitution. In 1789 he became the first president of the United States of America.

56
Abraham Lincoln
(served 1861-65)

Honest Abe's vision, courage, and integrity set him apart among America's presidents. It was his unflinching leadership that held the young nation together during the Civil War. To this day, his towering figure serves to remind us of the importance of personal responsibility and vigilance against the enemies of freedom.

57
Franklin Delano Roosevelt (served 1933-45)

After his "New Deal" economic program lifted America from the economic morass of the Great Depression, Roosevelt galvanized the nation into joining World War II's great fight against Nazi Germany and the Japanese Empire. Despite the fact that he was crippled by polio at the age of 39, FDR went on to become the longest serving president in US history. FDR's legacy can be understood in his famed Four Freedoms: freedom of speech, freedom of worship, freedom from want, and freedom from fear.

58
Thomas Jefferson (served 1801-09)

The man who penned the Declaration of Independence, Jefferson was a passionate and relentless promoter of the basic freedoms and rights guaranteed by the Constitution. During his presidency, the United States territory doubled in size, thanks to the Louisiana Purchase, a bold and favorable real estate deal negotiated with France in 1803. Jefferson sent Lewis and Clark on their Voyage of Discovery to explore the newly purchased land.

59
Dwight D. Eisenhower (served 1953-61)

Less than 10 years after he led the 1944 liberation of Europe, Dwight D. Eisenhower presided over nearly a decade of peace and prosperity. America had become the world's first modern superpower. The Eisenhower era was both the "Happy Days" and the era of the House Un-American Activities Committee (HUAC) investigations, the Red scare, and McCarthyism. It was a time of deceptive innocence and conformism, which led to the anti-establishment backlash and civil rights movement in the 1960s.

60
Ronald Reagan (served 1981-88)

A deep-seated belief in America's traditional values of freedom and free enterprise and the political courage to stand up for them were Ronald Reagan's greatest strengths. Among his most significant legacies are the peaceful resolution to the four-decade cold war with the Soviet Union and the Tax Reform Act of 1986.

61
Theodore Roosevelt
(served 1901-09)
*A foe of political corruption and big
industrial monopolies, Theodore
"Teddy" Roosevelt, age 42, was the
youngest president to take office up to
that time. He loved nature,
especially the West, and created the
Forest Service, setting aside
194 million acres of land and
forest for conservation.*

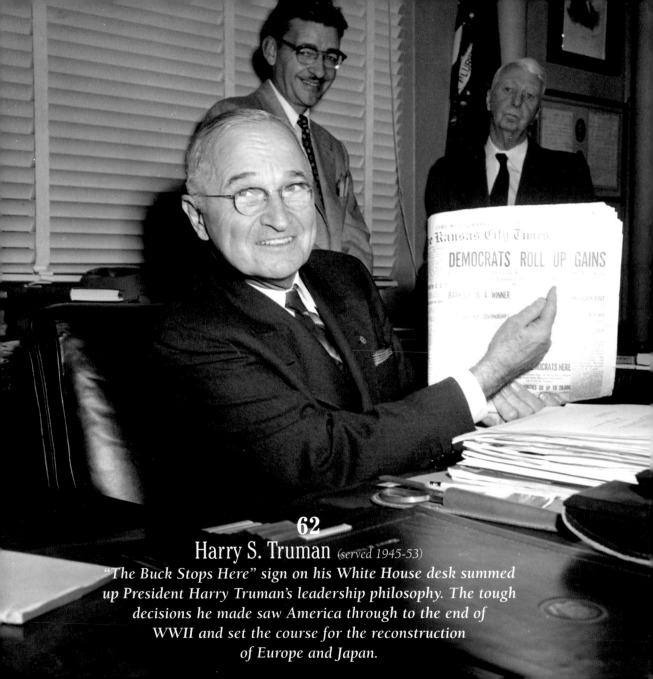

62
Harry S. Truman (served 1945-53)
*"The Buck Stops Here" sign on his White House desk summed
up President Harry Truman's leadership philosophy. The tough
decisions he made saw America through to the end of
WWII and set the course for the reconstruction
of Europe and Japan.*

63
James Knox Polk *(served 1845-49)*

Perhaps the hardest-working man ever to serve in the White House, Polk achieved the annexation of Texas, the conquest of the Southwest through a victorious war with Mexico, and the acquisition of Oregon from Britain. By the end of his single term, American power and influence rivaled that of Europe.

64
Andrew Jackson *(served 1829-37)*

Nicknamed "Old Hickory" for his toughness and steadfast character, he was the first president to be born in a log cabin. He used the powers of the presidency to empower the common man. He wanted to see "the people rule."

PIONEERS, PATRIOTS & LEGENDS

Americans celebrate the lives and the stories
of countless legendary men and women.

65 Benjamin Franklin (1706-1790)

*Franklin served the colonies as postmaster and
foreign ambassador, helped draft the Declaration of
Independence, and was a world-famous scientist
and inventor, making key discoveries about
electricity.*

66 Patrick Henry (1736-1799)

*A political leader in the American Revolution and a
well-known orator, Patrick Henry is famous for his
declarations, "If this be treason, make the most of
it," and "I know not what course others may take;
but as for me, give me liberty or give me death!"*

67 Paul Revere (1735-1818)

*This patriot made the famous horseback ride from
Boston to Concord during the night of April 18-19,
1775, to warn Massachusetts towns that the British
army was coming. Eighty years later, it was com-
memorated by Henry Wadsworth Longfellow in his
poem "Paul Revere's Ride."*

68 William F. Cody (1846-1917)

*The legendary Buffalo Bill Cody began to dazzle
audiences in 1883 with "Buffalo Bill's Wild West
Show"— a new form of arena entertainment which
traveled to small towns as well as cities.*

69 Thomas "Stonewall" Jackson (1824-1863)
A stalwart confederate leader in the Civil War. In the first battle of the war, an officer declared, "There is Jackson, standing like a stone wall!" The nickname stuck.

70 Betsy Ross (1752-1836)
An American seamstress born in Philadelphia, she is known to have made flags during the American Revolution, although the long-accepted story that she designed and made the first American national flag (the Stars & Stripes) is generally discredited.

71 Nathan Hale (1755-1776)
In 1776, this 21-year-old schoolteacher volunteered to investigate British troop strength in New York City. He was captured and hanged. His last words became an inspiring motto for U.S. patriots: "I regret that I have but one life to give for my country."

72 Samuel Adams (1722-1803)
Adams was called the "Firebrand of the American Revolution." He called for Committees of Correspondence in every colony, and by 1774 these committees had built a sense of national unity through the exchange of news and ideas.

73 Casey Jones (1864-1900)
Jones, who boasted that he always brought his train in on schedule, was an engineer on the Cannon Ball express from Memphis, Tennessee, to Canton, Mississippi. On April 30, 1900, at Vaughan, Mississippi, a stationary freight train appeared on the tracks ahead of his speeding locomotive. Although Casey applied the brakes, the Cannon Ball crashed and Jones died, but the passengers were saved. This event inspired a popular ballad.

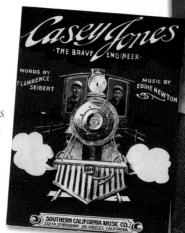

74 Johnny Appleseed (1774-1845)

John Chapman, an American pioneer, gave saplings and apple seeds to families migrating westward. For over 40 years, he wandered through Ohio, Indiana, and western Pennsylvania, visiting his forest nurseries and helping hundreds of settlers to establish orchards, thus earning the name "Johnny Appleseed."

75 Daniel Boone (1732-1820)

Along with other pioneers, Boone blazed trails and led pioneers into the western wilderness even before the Revolution. In 1775, he joined Indian trails together to create the Wilderness Road.

76 Rosie the Riveter

Rosie became a favorite wartime symbol of women ably taking over men's jobs during the early years of America's entrance into World War II. Six million women were added to the work force.

77 Davy Crockett (1786-1836)

This famous frontiersman was among the 100 Texans who were killed on March 6, 1836, defending their settlement against 5,000 Mexican troops in a battle known as the Siege of the Alamo. During the armed conflicts that followed, Texans, inspired by the rallying cry "Remember the Alamo!", prevailed. In September, the Republic of Texas was formed.

78 Wyatt Earp (1848-1929)

Earp was the most famous lawman of the Old West. His reputation was made by popular fiction and later by television. The only gunfight in which he was involved was the notorious "Gunfight at the O.K. Corral" in Arizona, in which three men were killed.

79 Deadwood Dick (1854-1921)

Nat Love, a former slave from Tennessee, became famous as a rodeo star called Deadwood Dick. African-American cowboys were common in the Old West. About one in seven cowboys was African-American, many of them former slaves.

80 Big Foot or Sasquatch

Described as a human-like creature 6 to 8 feet tall, covered with long, dark hair. Sightings and alleged encounters, as well as footprints, have been reported, mostly in the Pacific Northwest. (Also known as the abominable snowman, or Yeti, in the perpetual snow region of the Himalayas.)

81 Paul Bunyan

A legendary American lumberjack, he was the hero of a series of "tall tales" popular through the timber country from Michigan westward. Known for his fantastic strength and gigantic size, his prized possession was Babe the Blue Ox, the distance between whose horns measured 42 ax handles and a plug of tobacco.

82 Wild Bill Hickok (1837-1876)

Hickok was one of the few lawmen who was truly a great shot. It was said he rarely had to draw his gun because of his reputation for quickness and accuracy. He was killed in the mining town of Deadwood, Dakota Territory— shot in the back while playing poker. "Calamity Jane" was buried next to him years later. A crack shot herself, she encouraged the myth that she and Hickok were secretly married.

83 Calamity Jane (1852-1903)

Martha Jane Cannary of Princeton, Missouri, earned a reputation in the Wild West of being a fearless, self-sufficient woman of the frontier. She was fond of dressing in men's clothing after having donned a soldier's uniform while working for the army as a scout. Later, she traveled the west, carried mail for the pony express, and appeared in Buffalo Bill's Wild West Show displaying her riding and shooting abilities.

26 *Calamity Jane, Notorious Frontier Character.*
Gen. Crook's Scout.

REGISTER

5th

84
Uncle Sam

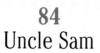

*Originally based on businessman
Samuel Wilson of Troy, New York,
Uncle Sam made his most famous
appearance on a WWI army recruiting
poster by James Montgomery Flagg.*

CITY FARM
GARD GARDENS

DON'T WAIT
for the Draft
VOLUNTEER

ASSOCIATED MOTION PICTURE ADVERTISERS, inc. Poster No. 3

GUENTHER

NTS OF JOSEPH H. TOOKER

The American Experience

America is a mix of carhops and cowboy hats and classic television shows; diners and drive-ins and homecoming parades. The star-spangled banner hanging from the front porch, hot-dogs at the ballgame, the sweet fragrance of spice and cinnamon potpourri during the Holidays. The fabric of American life is woven with a million experiences, images, and sounds.

LIVING IN THE USA

Everyday life in America is a mix of images, activities, sounds, and memories. Our diversity is reflected in our choice of fashion, favorite eats and language.

85
Wide, wraparound front porches
where we sit and talk and
watch the world go by

86
The general store, where the floor
boards creak, the shelves are dusty,
and you can buy candy by the pound and
pickles from the barrel

87
The barber shop, a place to share
fish stories and hear the
latest news

88
Adirondack chairs on a lakeside dock

89
Small-town main streets
lined with cars

90
A big red barn in a distant field

91
The importance
of family

92
Summertime roadside stands where
the whole family works

93
The Yankee Doodle shops in small New
England towns, where you can buy candles and
Christmas ornaments all year long

94
Classic wooden boats on a northern lake

95
A row of mailboxes at the end of a dirt road

96
Drive-in movies

97
Kelly green John Deere tractors

98
Handmade quilts handed down
through generations

Full-service gas stations
with free air

100
Displaying the flag
with pride on the
Fourth of July

101 Stratocaster electric guitars

102 The American flag painted on the side of a barn

103 A rusting pickup truck abandoned in a field

104 White picket fences in old New England towns

105 All-night laundromats

106 Harley Davidson motorcycles: an American icon of freedom and individuality

107 Holding up hometown signs for the TV camera at the *Today Show*

108 Pirate-themed miniature golf

109 Bumper stickers announcing political sentiments, animal rights, tourist destinations and school tuition issues

110 Springtime tag sales with children's toys, last year's shoes, old golf clubs and the Encyclopedia Britannica spread across the yard

111 Homecoming parades

112 Surfing and all things surf

113 A trip to the country to pick apples in the fall

114 Earning a merit badge in the local Boy Scout troop

115 The drive-through car wash with the blue light that flashes when the wax sprayer goes on

116 Home delivery of pizza and Chinese food

117 Hanging out at the local bowling alley

118 Pancake breakfast fund-raisers

119 Ordering winter clothes from the L.L. Bean catalog

120 The enthusiasm of majorettes and marching bands in a small town parade

128
The prom

142
Getting a new
Easter outfit

Kick it to the left!
Kick it to the right!
Stand up! Sit down!
Fight! Fight! Fight!

Thanksgiving Greetings

THANKSGIVING GREETINGS

158 Colorful Indian corn hanging on the front door in the fall

159 Watching the Macy's Thanksgiving Day parade while cooking Thanksgiving dinner

160 Spending the afternoon on the couch watching football games

161 Turkey soup, turkey sandwiches, and turkey pot pie, turkey basters, turkey lifters, turkey roasting pans, and a week's worth of turkey leftovers

162
The spectacular Rockettes
performing in the annual
Radio City Music Hall
Christmas show

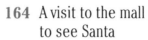

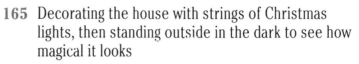

173
White bread
sandwiches
with a big glass
of milk

CLASSIC AMERICAN FOOD

The simplicity and heartiness of our traditional recipes seem to ensure their survival despite diets and imported delicacies. And what's more American than apple pie?

YOU DON'T KNOW BEANS UNTIL YOU COME TO BOSTON, MASS.

BUNKER HILL BEANS STATE HOUSE

STATE SEAL

WASHINGTON

APPLES

DISTRIBUTED *Exclusively by* PACIFIC FRUIT & PRODUCE CO.

206
Washington State
apples

207
Idaho Potatoes

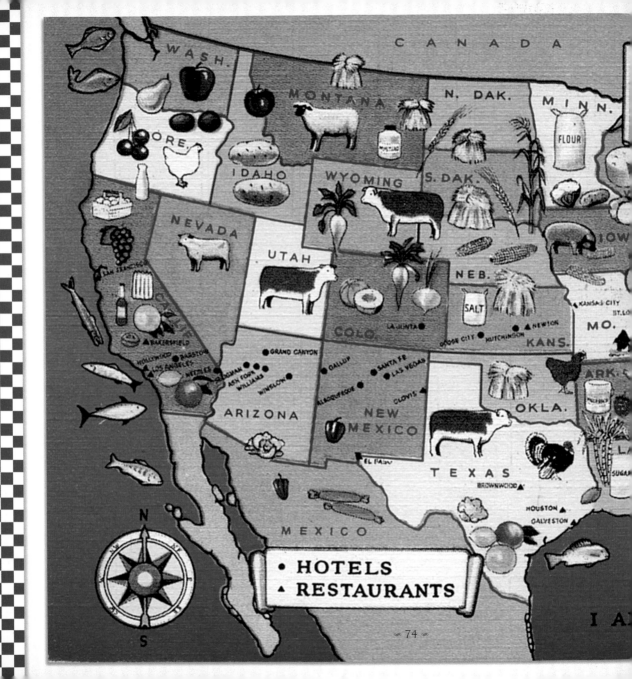

220 Popsicles

Invented in 1905 by 11-year-old Frank Epperson, they were originally called "Epsicles." The twin Popsicle came out during the Depression years.

221 TV dinners

The first TV dinner was introduced in 1954 by Swanson & Sons. It was roast turkey with stuffing and gravy, sweet potatoes and peas. It cost 98 cents and came in a box that looked like a television set.

**222
Oreo**

This great American cookie was invented in 1912.

223 Julia Child

Julia Child's influence on American cooking can't be measured. Her first book, Mastering the Art of French Cooking (1961), brought the exotic and refined recipies of France into kitchens more accustomed to Betty Crocker. Child's influence spread further with her PBS television series, The French Chef. In 2001, Julia Child donated her entire kitchen to the Smithsonian's National Museum of American History in Washington. Bon appétit!

224 James Beard

Chef, author, teacher, television personality, founder of The James Beard Cooking School and inspiration for The James Beard Foundation, a group dedicated to preserving the culinary heritage of America, Beard has often been called The Father of American Cooking.

225 Stuffed celery

4 CELERY STALKS
1 JAR OF KRAFT CHEESE SPREAD WITH PIMIENTOS
Wash and cut up the celery into 4-inch sections. Spread the cheese in the middle, level with the top of the celery. Enjoy.

226 Grits with everything

St. George, South Carolina, The Grits Capital of the World, hosts the annual World Grits Festival each April. The beauty of grits is that they can be enjoyed at any meal and are enhanced by butter, gravy, cheese, or anything your heart desires.

227 Fortune cookies

These treats are believed to have been invented at San Francisco's Japanese Tea Garden in Golden Gate Park in 1914 by Makato Hagiwara.

228 tuna noodle casserole

Invented in the 1940s, it was a staple throughout the 1950s at potluck suppers.
Cook some flat egg noodles and place in casserole dish. Pour a can of Campbell's Cream of Mushroom soup and a half cup of milk over noodles. Add a package of frozen peas and a 12-oz. Can of tuna, drained, and stir. Bake for 20 minutes at 400 degrees. Crush some saltine crackers and sprinkle on top. Bake five more minutes until lightly browned.

Expect the unexpected.

229 The Joy of Cooking

Author Irma Rombauer was neither a good cook nor an experienced writer, and yet her classic cookbook is still in print today. Casual, friendly, full of simple information and short-cuts, Rombauer focused on the "joy," which is perhaps why the book has remained popular for over 70 years.

230 Caesar salad
Invented by chef Caesar Cardini on the Fourth of July weekend, 1924.

231 Cobb salad
Invented in 1926 at The Brown Derby Restaurant in Los Angeles and named after Bob Cobb.

232 Waldorf salad
Invented by Oscar of the Waldorf for the opening of the Waldorf Astoria Hotel on March 9, 1896.

233 Thousand Island dressing
George and Sophia LaLonde of Clayton, New York first created this popular salad dressing in the early 1900's.

234 Ranch dressing
Salad dressing invented in the 1950's at Hidden Valley Guest Ranch Resort in California.

235 A triple venti non-fat caramel macchiato at Starbucks

236 Great American beers: Pabst Blue Ribbon, Hamms, Rolling Rock, Coors, Miller's, Sam Adams and Budweiser

237 Manhattans, Long Island Ice Tea, Americanos, Martinis

238 Pepsi Cola

239 Stewart's Root Beer and Vernor's ginger ale

240 Dr Pepper
Invented by pharmacist Charles Alderton in Waco, Texas, in 1885.

241 Coca Cola
Coca Cola was invented by Atlanta pharmacist John Pemberton and was sold to the public for the first time on May 8, 1886.

242 Bologna sandwiches on white bread

243 Creamed chipped beef on toast

244 Fig Newtons

245 Life Savers

Michael Stefanos, creator of the Dove Bar, and his mother, Sophia, making magic at the original Dove Candies location in Chicago, 1984

246
Dove Bars

It sure hits the spot!

THE AMERICAN RESTAURANT

The great variety of offerings in dining establishments
across the country reflect our diversity and the
melting pot of cultures. Where else in the world can you go into a
restaurant at 4:00 am and order eggplant parmigiana, souvlaki,
chicken kiev or nachos all from the same enormous menu?

258
Classic American diners
that stay open all night

259
Giant sandwiches at
a New York deli

260
A dim sum lunch in a restaurant in
San Francisco's Chinatown

261
The festive atmosphere of
local brew pubs

262
Ice cream parlors and
soda fountains

263
Hearty dinners
at Amish restaurants

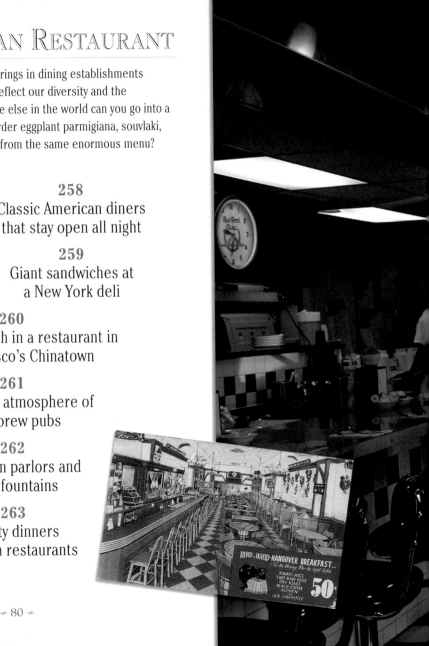

264
Getting a booth by the
window with a view of
the parking lot

BUCKEYE DINER
MEDINA, OHIO

DiLEGO'S DINER

North Adams, Mass.

265
The distinctive streamlined style of the American diner

TRENT DINER

AMPLE PARKING SPACE—AIR CONDITIONED
TRENT DINER · Trenton, N.J. Route U.S. No.1

YANKEE FLYER
THE PLACE TO EAT
236 MAIN ST.   NASHUA, N.H.

To DINE at WIGHTMAN'S is to DINE WELL
WIGHTMAN'S DINER
Boston Post Road,   So. Attleboro, Mass.

CAESAR'S

Lancaster Pike & Norwood Ave.
ROSEMONT, PENNA.

MILLER'S TWINDINER

DINER

RIVERHEAD
LONG ISLAND

272 SOUTH ST.   104 ORISKANY ST. EAST
UTICA, N.Y.   UTICA, N.Y.
Jack & Andy Diners
23 GENESEE ST.   128 N. GENESEE ST.
NEW HARTFORD, N.Y.   UTICA, N.Y.

CLEAN SERVICE   QUALITY FOOD
AVON GRILL   AVON GRILL
3343 READING RD, CINCINNATI, OHIO

Quality Food   Quick Service
DINER DINER
HAZEMONT DINER
OUTER HAMMOND STREET
BANGOR, MAINE

SCRATCH MY BACK
MARYLAND MATCH CO.
BALTO., MD. MADE IN U.S.A.
KLESS DINER
JUNCTION OF MORRIS—MILLBURN AVES. UNION N.J.

The Place to Eat   236 MAIN ST.
NASHUA, N.H.
YANKEE FLYER

LEXINGTON
DINER
and DINING ROOM
On Route 309 Half

JOHN'S
ROUTE 25

PAU
STATE · HI
GAT

THE WORLD
Quality Food for you

TURN OVER FOR
STRIKING SURFACE
24 HOUR

QUICK SERVICE
A REAL PL
Diner
B

WIND GAP, PA.
ROUTE 12 AND 115   "The Gateway to the Poconos"...

MERCER "air conditioned" DINER
BREAKFAST
LUNCHES - FULL COURSE DINNERS • Phone MERCER 9392
LEO McMONAGLE - T. N. CLAYTON, PROP'S.

DINER
AMBOY AVE.

THE ORIGINAL
Effort Diner
PENNSYLVANIA
DUTCH COOKING
"the Poconos Finest"
ROUTE 115 — EFFORT, PA.
Phone: SAylorsburg 16814
MADE IN U.S.A.
Effort Diner

OPEN
24 HRS
A DAY   ALL BAKING DONE ON THE PREMISES   AIR-CONDITIONED
BAYONNE DINER
226 BROADWAY at 9TH
FEDERAL 9-9822   BAYONNE, N.J.

DINER

On the White Horse Pike
JOE'S DINER   EGG HARBOR N.J.
JOE'S DINER
NEVER CLOSED   Established 1921

Rippowam Grill   ON BOSTON POST ROAD STAMFORD, CONN.
BOOTH
and
COUNTER
SERVICE
PARKING
SPACE   ALWAYS OPEN

ECAUCUS, N. J.
TURNPIKE

MORAN SQ. DINER
Moran Sq. Diner
FITCHBURG   Tel. 514   MASS.

AIR CONDITIONED • OPEN 24 HOURS
GIBERSON'S DINER
phone MI-1-2422 • FOOD FIT FOR A KING
INTERSECTING ROUTES 9-40 & 322
BLACK HORSE PIKE & NEW ROAD, PLEASANTVILLE, N.J.   125 SEATS

1212 Madison Ave.
Paterson, N. J.
UTIFUL DINER
tioned for your Comfort

The Diner of 1999
HUDSON VALLEY VENDING CO.
TEL. 779 - 314 N. BROADWAY
N. TARRYTOWN • • • N.Y.
Eat the Dining Car Way

DUFF'S DINER   FRONT ROYAL, VA.
Owned & Operated by
L. W. LUTTRELL

Diner
BEVERLY, MASS.

YANKEE FLYER
THE PLACE TO EAT   236 MAIN ST.
NASHUA, N. H.

Bridge Diner   BRIDGE SEA GRILL
BRIDGE DINER
NEW BEDFORD AND FAIRHAVEN BRIDGE
NEW BEDFORD, MASS.

QUALITY FOOD
NER
LVD.

TRIANGLE Diner
TRIANGLE DINER
U.S. HIGHWAYS 11-17-50 & 522, WINCHESTER, VA.

AIR CONDITIONED   OPEN 24 HOURS
DICK'S DINER

Without giving up the semi-private world of their automobile interior, motorists could summon service simply by flashing their headlights or depressing the switch on a speaker-box. In a flash an eager carhop would arrive—perhaps dressed in a colorful majorette uniform—or in some instances, sporting roller skates. Gliding across the asphalt with a tray full of hamburgers, French fries, and milkshakes, the curb-girl was an unforgettable sight.

Philip Langdon,
Forward to The All-American Drive-In Restaurant

STEAK n SHAKE
GENUINE CHILI   TRU - FLAVOR SHAKES

266
The Drive-in

267
Carhop

277
Restaurant & Diner lingo

Adam and Eve on a raft: *two poached eggs on toast*

Bullets: *baked beans*

Burn one: *throw a burger on the grill*

Zepplins in a fog: *sausages with mashed potatoes*

Whisky down: *rye toast*

Cremate a blue, bikini cut: *a well-toasted blueberry muffin divided into four pieces*

Hemorrhage: *ketchup*

Full house: *grilled cheese with bacon and tomato*

Cluck and grunt: *eggs and bacon*

The twins: *salt and pepper*

Noah's boy: *A slice of ham (Ham was one of Noah's sons...)*

278 Horn & Hardart's Automats

Part cafeteria, part assembly line, part fast-food operation, the Automat debuted in Philadelphia in 1902 and quickly became a success. Automats served 800,000 people a day during their peak years. The last one closed in New York in 1991, and today a 35-foot section of the original Philadelphia restaurant resides in the Smithsonian's National Museum of American History.

279 The 21 Club, New York

Thirty-two cast iron jockeys line the façade of the famous 21. It began life as a speakeasy during Prohibition and today is an elegant place where the elite meet to eat.

280
Howard Johnson's Restaurants and Motor Lodges

Founded in 1925 by Howard Dearing Johnson of Massachusetts, the orange-roofed HoJos restaurants dominated American highways during the 1940s and 1950s, serving reliable food like steaks, chops, chicken and their famous fried clam strips. Howard Johnson's was also famous for having 28 flavors of ice cream.

Two or Three Cups of Coffee

Coffee is coffee in New England. Coffee is fine in New York and Pennsylvania. Southerners make exceptional coffee sometimes; it's a ritual in Charleston and  a religion in New Orleans. But when you head west, something happens, something insidious, stealthy, treacherous. Independence, Missouri, is about where you begin to notice it. By the time you've crossed the river into Kansas, there can be no mistake. You have two or three cups of coffee for breakfast in Topeka and notice that your heart isn't started yet. By the time you get to Denver, the stuff doesn't smell or taste like coffee. At Grand Junction it doesn't look like coffee. Cross the Wasatch Mountains into Salt Lake, and there's nothing to do but buy yourself a coffeepot and brew your own. There's nothing resembling coffee to be had in a café until you reach the Sierras and drop down toward Sacramento.

Probably there's a historical basis for this. The pioneers, pushing off across the Missouri River, quickly ran out of coffee and had to start reusing the same grounds. Their children grew up liking it that way. The Mormon pioneers who peopled Salt Lake City rejected coffee as a brew of the devil, and their descendants figure, apparently, that if they aren't going to drink coffee around here, neither is anybody else.

Californians, of course, got fresh supplies by schooner around the Horn, so California coffee remained drinkable. But from Kansas City to Reno, when the waitress says in the morning, "Would you like a cup of coffee?" I smile and  nod and watch glumly what she pours into the cup and say to myself, "Oh, would I ever!" Salt Lake City coffee is America's weakest. Some say Brookings, South Dakota, but they are people who haven't been to Salt Lake City.

Charles Kuralt, *Dateline America, 1979*

281
A big breakfast at the coffee
shop with eggs, bacon, toast,
pancakes, maple syrup, and
the bottomless coffee cup

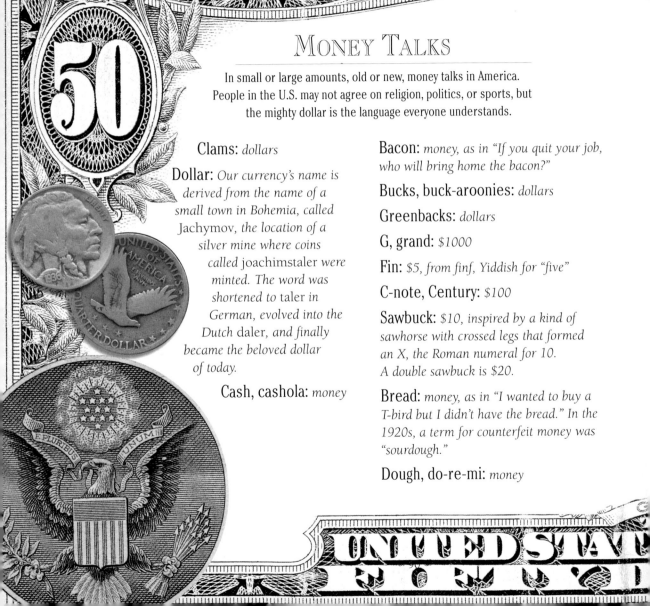

MONEY TALKS

In small or large amounts, old or new, money talks in America.
People in the U.S. may not agree on religion, politics, or sports, but
the mighty dollar is the language everyone understands.

Clams: *dollars*

Dollar: *Our currency's name is derived from the name of a small town in Bohemia, called* Jachymov, *the location of a silver mine where coins called* joachimstaler *were minted. The word was shortened to* taler *in German, evolved into the Dutch* daler, *and finally became the beloved dollar of today.*

Cash, cashola: *money*

Bacon: *money, as in "If you quit your job, who will bring home the bacon?"*

Bucks, buck-aroonies: *dollars*

Greenbacks: *dollars*

G, grand: *$1000*

Fin: *$5, from finf, Yiddish for "five"*

C-note, Century: *$100*

Sawbuck: *$10, inspired by a kind of sawhorse with crossed legs that formed an X, the Roman numeral for 10. A double sawbuck is $20.*

Bread: *money, as in "I wanted to buy a T-bird but I didn't have the bread." In the 1920s, a term for counterfeit money was "sourdough."*

Dough, do-re-mi: *money*

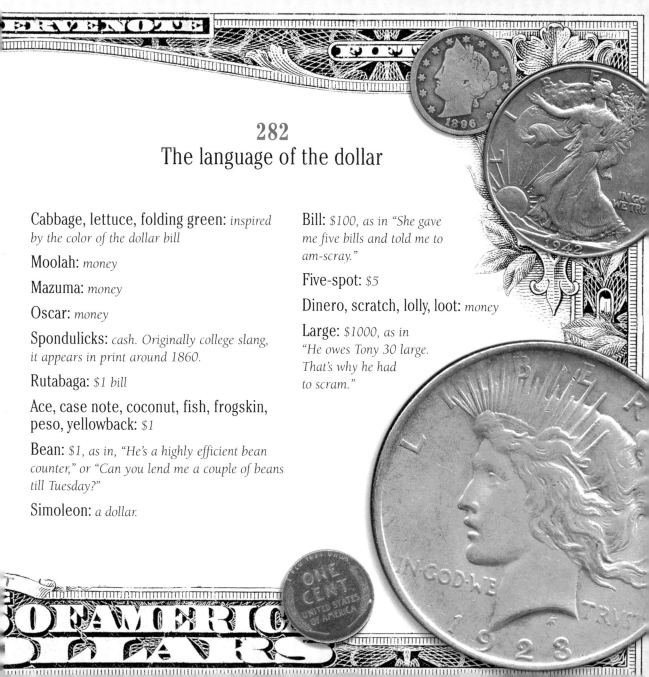

282
The language of the dollar

Cabbage, lettuce, folding green: *inspired by the color of the dollar bill*

Moolah: *money*

Mazuma: *money*

Oscar: *money*

Spondulicks: *cash. Originally college slang, it appears in print around 1860.*

Rutabaga: *$1 bill*

Ace, case note, coconut, fish, frogskin, peso, yellowback: *$1*

Bean: *$1, as in, "He's a highly efficient bean counter," or "Can you lend me a couple of beans till Tuesday?"*

Simoleon: *a dollar.*

Bill: *$100, as in "She gave me five bills and told me to am-scray."*

Five-spot: *$5*

Dinero, scratch, lolly, loot: *money*

Large: *$1000, as in "He owes Tony 30 large. That's why he had to scram."*

Sounds of Spring

The words fairly waft out of Florida on warm, orange-scented zephyrs. They are the language of baseball, cliches describing spring training, an event that is itself a cliche, conjuring up fascinating visions …

"…The Grapefruit League campaign…the longest stint by a Tiger hurler this spring…the slender southpaw…the long blast was the rookie's second homer in as many contests…the skipper said he intends to use the big right-handed slugger mostly against left-handed pitchers this season…'The kid's playing his way into a job. I think we'll take him north with us. He's got a good set of wheels and he can go to his left'…It was the fast-baller's first outing of the spring…"

They are the sounds of this season and last season and the season 10 years ago and the season a thousand years ago, as unchanging as the immutable game itself.

They are interspersed with imagined noises like the crack of a bat, the pop of a well-thrown ball smacking into a glove, the hen-clucking of the catcher squatting there in his armor, the ancient litany of the players afield, the clatter of spikes on dugout steps, the soft thud of tobacco juice in the dust, all of the ritualistic noises of the summer game.

It is spellbinding, this news from the training camps, for buried somewhere in all of it is the secret of the future, embryonic pennant winners, the rookies who will not wilt under the spotlight, the veterans who will falter or find new glory.

283
Spring training, the harbinger of baseball

We listen, trying to sort through the multitude of sounds for some sign that the Yankees will reign again, that the Phillies have found some help for Carlton, that the madman Durocher can still manage a Champion, that the Braves finally have some pitching...

But that's all we get, really, signs, like a catcher's signal to a pitcher. There is no assurance that the curve won't hang. (Every home run ever hit was off a hanging curve, if the pitchers are telling the truth.)

These distant events are reassuring, though. They are rustles of springtime, warm breezes blowing through the gray chill as winter exits snapping and snarling. Even as the cold rain drums on the windows, we can feel the sun raising beads of sweat to be wiped away with the back of a glove when we read, "Lee May singled, doubled, then slammed a 450-foot two-run homer off Lew Krausse..."

....This is spring training and reality has not yet set in for the year. The homers are being struck off winter-softened arms. The hitless innings are being hurled against eyes not yet focused on the snake-slide curveball. The standings are myths.

But spring training is not a time for reality. It is a time for speculation, anticipation, hope, a soft time when things don't really count, when we only imagine they do.

Ron Green, Sounds of Spring, 1973

AMERICAN SOUNDS, AMERICAN SMELLS

The plink of a banjo on a hot summer night, the fragrance of mulled cider at Christmas, the squeak of sneakers on the basketball court— these distinctive sounds and smells may go unnoticed, but they are a vivid part of the American experience.

284 The distant bells of the Good Humor truck on a summer evening

285 A chorus of frogs announcing the beginning of spring in a New Jersey swamp

286 The cheer that rises from the bleachers after a home run

287 The daily ringing of the opening bell on Wall Street

288 The beloved kazoo

289 The "ding ding" of the San Francisco cable car bell

Bowling

290 The sound of a strike in the local bowling alley

291 The rattling and rumbling of a New York subway train

292 The stirring sound of a marching band

293 The cheer that rises from the crowd when the hometown football team takes the field

294 The call of a bird in swamps, forests, parks and fields

295 The roll of distant thunder that announces the arrival of the monsoons in the Arizona desert

296 A lonesome train whistle in the night

297 The cry "All aboard!" on an Amtrak train

298 The dry crunch of snow under your feet as you walk across a frozen Minnesota lake

299 The Cajun accordion and country fiddle

300 The rush of wind through the palm trees in Key West

301 Tap dancing

302 Banjos

303 Church bells on Sunday morning

304 Cartoon sounds like bop, bam, wham, whack, and the whistling sound of Wiley Coyote falling off a high desert cliff

305 The ringing sound of money, hopes, and dreams echoing through a Las Vegas casino

306 The soft lowing of cattle on a Montana ranch

307 The cries of seagulls following a ferryboat across the Puget Sound

308 The barking of seals lounging off the coast of California

309 The crackling of campfires on a dark Arkansas October night

310 The organ playing old songs at skating rinks

311 A celebrity singing the *Star Spangled Banner* at the opening of a big baseball game

312 The smack sound of a basketball bouncing on a gymnasium floor

313 Sneakers squeaking on a gym floor

314 The explosive roar of drag racing

315 The incessant repetition of drivetime news radio

316 The sound of Morse code on a telegraph

317 The eerie call of a loon on a northern lake

"Sweet Adeline! My Adeline!" "For you I pine, for you I pine!"

318 The crack of the bat when it hits the baseball

319 The umpire calling "Strike one!"

320 A giant American flag snapping in the wind

321 The roar of the powerful surf along the beach in California and Hawaii

322 The roar of Harley Davidson motorcycles

323 The dry song of the washboard

Two over easy!

324 The call of the waitress in an all night truck stop

325 Boogity, boogity, boogity: the sound of NASCAR

326 Barbershop quartets

327 The beep-beep sound of the cartoon Roadrunner

328 The often imitated sounds of the Three Stooges

329 The howl of a wolf deep in the forest

330 The sizzle and pop of eggs hitting the griddle in a small town diner

331 The unsettling sound of ketchup exiting a squeeze bottle at a diner

332 The clatter of a can of soda falling into the bottom of the coin-operated soda machine

333 The distant pops and cracks of fireworks on the 4th of July

334 The mellow sound of the Hawaiian steel guitar

335 The organ music that punctuates the innings of a baseball game

336 The "pffft" sound that accompanies the opening of a can of Budweiser

337 The sirens of emergency vehicles on a hot summer night in the city

338 Traditional New Orleans jazz

339 The whistle of a big paddle wheel riverboat coming around the bend

340 The melancholy sound of a harmonica on a summer night

341 Popcorn at the movie theater

342 Cinnabons at the airport

343 The intense, refreshing smell of pines when you get out of the car after a long drive up to the cabin in the north woods of Michigan

344 The heady smell of eucalyptus in California

345 The strong aroma of pizza in O'Hare airport when you get off the plane

346 Fresh baked doughnuts

347 Turkey roasting in the oven on Thanksgiving

348 Mulled cider at Christmas

349 The fragrance of gardenias in the South

350 The sweet orange blossoms of southern California orchards

351 The salty sea air in Maine

352 The overwhelming smell of Bloomingdale's perfume department

353 The fragrance of piñon and sage burning in the kivas of Santa Fe and Taos, New Mexico

354 The rich, mouth-watering aromas of garlic, oregano, basil, tomato and cheese that linger in an old neighborhood Italian restaurant

355 The sense of possibility that comes with the smell of a new car

Baloney, Cooties & 23 Skidoo

America's words and expressions are a reflection of our diversity, dynamism, and willingness to embrace the new and interesting... Cool!

356
The evolving American language

gorm: *to eat with enthusiasm (1850)*

smouge: *to cheat or steal (1850)*

23 Skidoo!: *a popular phrase that could mean almost anything (ca. 1910)*

airedale: *a less-than-attractive gentleman (1920s)*

And how!: *a positive affirmation (1920s)*

baloney: *a word expressing disbelief; nonsense. Similar to hogwash, hooey, bunk, balderdash, poppycock, rubbish, and drivel. (1920s) As in, "Don't try to tell me pigs can fly. That's a load of baloney!"*

Hot dawg! Hot diggity dog! *An expression of enthusiasm. (1920s)*

whoopee: *fun (1920s)*

shindig: *a dance or party (1930s)*

hootenanny: *a gathering where folk songs are sung (1929)*

lollapalooza: *something extraordinary (1930s)*

groovy: *originating from the phrase "in the groove," a jazz term of the mid-1930s, groovy makes the scene in the 1940s. It reappears in the mid-1960s for a brief time before it is pronounced to have cooties.*

square: *someone or something that is not cool. "He is so square, he wears a pocket protector." (1940s)*

like, wow, man! *an expression of astonishment (1950s)*

cool: *Possibly the most-used word in the history of language; a positive, desirable state or quality of being (1950s)*

cooties: *an imaginary and unappealing quality related to undesirable people; possibly contagious. (1950s)*

gross, groady, rank, raunchy, scuzzy: *disgusting (1960s)*

Far out!: *something extraordinary (1960s)*

"It is to those days before the Civil War that we owe many of the colorful American terms for strong drink, still current, e.g., *panther-sweat, nose-paint, red-eye, corn-juice, forty-rod, mountain-dew, coffin-varnish, bust-head, stagger-soup, tonsil-paint, squirrel-whiskey*, and so on, and for drunk, e.g., *boiled, canned, cock-eyed, frazzled, fried, oiled, ossified, pifflicated, pie-eyed, plastered, snozzled, stewed, stuccoed, tanked, woozy*."

H.L. Menken, *The American Language*, 1937

out to lunch: *not in touch with current reality (1960s) As in, "What's he talkin' about, man? That freak is out to lunch!"*

talk to Ralph on the big white telephone: *to vomit (1970s)*

bodacious: *impressive; bold and audacious. First appearing in 1832, it became popular in the 1980s.*

dude: *a guy. First appearing in the 1870s, dude has grown from its original meaning of a fancy gentleman to its current meaning of a more familiar person. As in, "Hey, dude! Where's my car?"*

-meister: *derived from the German word meaning "master, it is used as a suffix added to nouns, verbs, adjectives and proper names to indicate an expertise, mastery or special affiliation. Usually preceded by "The." As in, The Donmeister, The Cheesemeister, The Beermeister, The Joggingmeister. (1990s)*

yesterday: *out of style; a has-been. As in, "I'm like, so over him. He is totally so yesterday." (1990s)*

been there, done that: *a dismissal indicating that the suggestion is so yesterday (1990s)*

sick: *cool (1990s). As in, "That car is so totally awesome, dude! That car is sick!"*

bomb diggity: *cool; the best (2000s)*

peace out: *goodbye (2000s)*

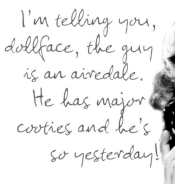

I'm telling you, dollface, the guy is an airedale. He has major cooties and he's so yesterday!

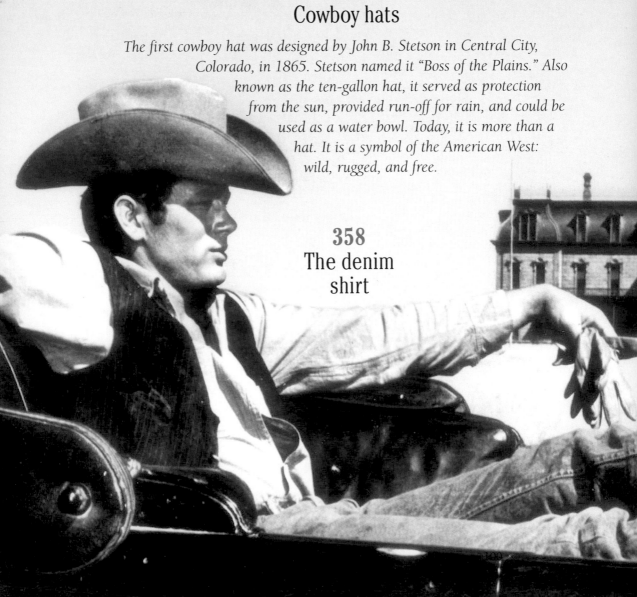

357
Cowboy hats

The first cowboy hat was designed by John B. Stetson in Central City, Colorado, in 1865. Stetson named it "Boss of the Plains." Also known as the ten-gallon hat, it served as protection from the sun, provided run-off for rain, and could be used as a water bowl. Today, it is more than a hat. It is a symbol of the American West: wild, rugged, and free.

358
The denim shirt

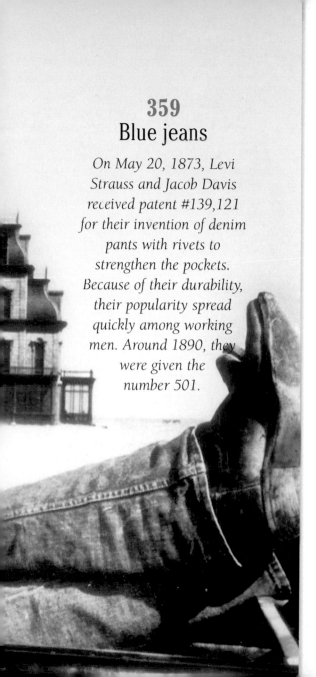

359
Blue jeans

On May 20, 1873, Levi Strauss and Jacob Davis received patent #139,121 for their invention of denim pants with rivets to strengthen the pockets. Because of their durability, their popularity spread quickly among working men. Around 1890, they were given the number 501.

AMERICAN STYLE

Americans wear their blue jeans and Brooks Brothers with pride and a unique sense of style.

360
Cowboy boots
Plain or fancy, they are truly an American classic.

361
The tuxedo
Introduced by the Lorillard family at the Autumn Ball of 1886 at the Tuxedo Club, Tuxedo Park, New York. Hence the name.

362
OshKosh overalls

363
Baseball caps with logos

364
Penny loafers

365
His and hers matching Hawaiian shirts

366
Two-toned bucks and bobby socks

367
Red and black lumberjack shirt

368
Black leather jackets with the collar turned up

369
Surferdude
shorts

JUNE 1945

390
The classic style
and grace of
Jacqueline Kennedy
Onassis

The First Lady visits the Parthenon in
Athens, Greece, June, 1961.

January 19, 1961,
Washington, D.C.

Gatherings, Groups & Get-togethers

We celebrate our individuality and our similarities in countless groups and organizations. Our Constitution's gift to us: Freedom of Assembly.

391
Boy Scouts of America

392
The Boys and Girls Clubs

393
The yearly summer gathering of airplane enthusiasts at the Experimental Aircraft Association fly-in in Oshkosh, Wisconsin

394
Star Trek conventions

395
The Democratic and Republican National Conventions

396
America gives us the freedom to gather with like-minded individuals who share our special interests

397

Garage bands

398
The Annual Sturgis
Motorcycle Rally,
Sturgis, South Dakota:
Founded by
J. Clarence "Pappy" Hoel
in 1939

399
The Burning Man Project

Over 25,000 people gather on Labor Day weekend to celebrate creativity, art, and individuality, culminating in the burning of a giant wooden statue of a man. Begun in San Francisco in 1986, the event moved to the Nevada desert in 1991. They are now the largest "Leave No Trace" gathering in the world, due to their diligent clean-up efforts at the end of the festival.

400
Civil War re-enactments

401
The Vent Haven International
Ventriloquists' ConVENTion

402
Pow wows

403
Woodstock, 1969

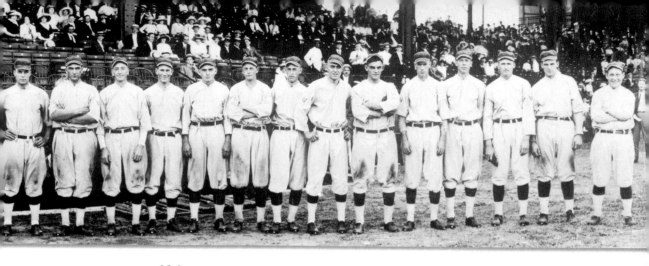

404
Model T Ford Club of America:
The World's Largest Model T Ford Club

405
Fan clubs, book clubs, knitting clubs

406
Baseball teams

407
Beauty pageants

AUTO
REPAIRING
ALL WORK GUARANTEED.
SERVICE
EP'T.
PLUMBING
426½

408
The Lions, the Elks,
the Masons, and
the Shriners

REFLECTIONS OF OURSELVES
GREAT AMERICAN MOVIES

Movies capture the classic American landscape, the romance
of the Wild West, small-town life and big city glamour,
and heroes that show us the best that we can be.

409 American Grafitti (1973)
*A glimpse of America during the innocent
summer of 1962.*

410 The Last Picture Show (1971)
*A film that shows us the uncertain future of a bleak,
dusty Texas town in the 1950s.*

411 Gone With The Wind (1939)
*Margaret Mitchell's epic tale of self-preservation
during the Civil War.*

**412 Charlie Chaplin's Little
Tramp movies** (Teens and '20s)
*He won the hearts of America as he
stood up to countless bullies.*

413 The Right Stuff (1983)
*Competing American astronauts inspire and
fulfill America's dream of space flight.*

414 Drums Along the Mohawk (1939)
*The struggle to survive at the edge of the
wilderness in Revolutionary times.*

415 The Babe Ruth Story (1948)
*The supreme hero of America's pastime knocks
them out of the park.*

416
High Noon (1952)

The classic American western starring
Gary Cooper as Marshal Will Kane.

417
It's a Wonderful Life (1946)

Frank Capra's all-time classic Christmas movie set in fictional Bedford Falls, New York.

424 Easy Rider (1969)

Dennis Hopper and Peter Fonda ride across America on classic motorcycles. Born to be wild!

425 The Graduate (1967)

A college graduate confronts issues of adult life, accompanied by Simon and Garfunkel.

426 Ordinary People (1980)

A family tragedy set in the northern suburbs of Chicago.

427 Shirley Temple movies (30's and 40's)

She enthralled the country with her curls, singing, and dancing. We watched her grow up on the silver screen as a typical American girl.

428 The Christmas Story (1983) **and Miracle on 34th Street** (1947)

American children and the meaning of Christmas.

429 The Deer Hunter (1978)

Vietnam changes young draftees from Pennsylvania forever.

430 The Public Enemy (1931)

Benchmark gangster movie starring Jimmy Cagney who gets involved in a Prohibition racket.

431 Knute Rockne, All American (1940)

First-generation American coach establishes his legend on the gridiron at Notre Dame, starring Pat O'Brien as Rockne and Ronald Reagan as "The Gipper."

432 Grapes of Wrath (1940)

The Joad family's struggle for survival during the Great Depression.

433 The Maltese Falcon (1941)

Based on the novel by Dashiell Hammett, Humphrey Bogart plays detective Sam Spade, who gets himself involved in more than he bargained for. A great example of American film noir's tough guy movies.

434 It Happened One Night (1934)

Perfect American story of fast-talking newsman getting his big story and also the rich heiress.

435 From Here to Eternity (1953)

American servicemen respond to the attack at Pearl Harbor.

436 On the Waterfront (1954)

Former fighter battles alone against corrupt union bosses on New York's waterfront and wins.

437 Rebel Without a Cause (1955)

James Dean, Sal Mineo, and Natalie Wood endure adolescent challenges in the 1950s.

438 The Best Years of Our Lives (1946)

Returning home to a small town after WWII, three veterans find that war has changed their lives forever.

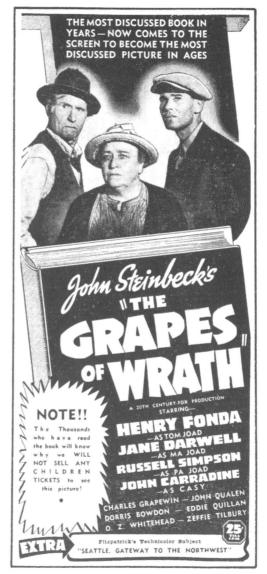

Clint Eastwood won two Oscars for best picture and best director for his 1992 film, "The Unforgiven."

439
Unforgettable American films

2001: A Space Odyssey
All About Eve
All the President's Men
American Beauty
Anatomy of a Murder
Annie Hall
Apocalypse Now
The Apartment
Apollo 13
Ben-Hur
Born Yesterday
Breaking Away
The Bridge on the River Kwai
Bringing Up Baby
Bullitt
Butch Cassidy and the
    Sundance Kid
Cabaret
Casablanca
Cat on a Hot Tin Roof
Citizen Kane
Chinatown
Clint Eastwood's Dirty Harry Films
Close Encounters of the Third Kind
The Color Purple
Cool Hand Luke
Dances with Wolves

Deliverance
Double Indemnity
Gone with the Wind
E.T. The Extra-Terrestrial
Fantasia, Bambi and Snow White
Father of the Bride
A Few Good Men
Finding Nemo
Five Easy Pieces
Forrest Gump
The Godfather
Guess Who's
    Coming to Dinner
High Society
Holiday Inn
The Hustler
Jaws
Key Largo
The Longest Day
M.A.S.H.
Midnight Cowboy
Mister Roberts
Mr. Smith Goes
    to Washington
The Music Man
Mutiny on the Bounty
National Velvet

Norma Rae
North by Northwest
Old Yeller
On Golden Pond
One Flew Over the Cuckoo's Nest
Patton
Philadelphia
The Philadelphia Story
Platoon
The Pride of the Yankees
Raging Bull
Raiders of the Lost Ark
Rain Man
Rocky
Saving Private Ryan
Schindler's List
Sergeant York
Shane
Singin' in the Rain
Some Like It Hot
A Star is Born
Star Wars
Steamboat Willie
The Sting
A Streetcar Named Desire
Sunset Boulevard
Taxi Driver
Thelma and Louise
Toy Story
The Unforgiven
West Side Story
Who's Afraid of Virginia Wolf?
The Wizard of Oz
Yankee Doodle Dandy
The Yearling

Jean Harlow, circa 1930

440
Hollywood's immortal actors

Bud Abbott & Lou Costello	George Burns
Gracie Allen	James Cagney
June Allyson	Eddie Cantor
Don Ameche	John Carradine
Dana Andrews	Leo G. Carroll
Fred Astaire	John Cassavetes
Gene Autry	Lon Chaney
Lew Ayres	Charles Chaplin
Lauren Bacall	Montgomery Clift
Lucille Ball	Glenn Close
Anne Bancroft	Lec J. Cobb
John Barrymore	James Coburn
Lionel Barrymore	Claudette Colbert
Warner Baxter	Ronald Colman
Warren Beatty	Gary Cooper
Wallace Beery	Jackie Cooper
Ralph Bellamy	Joseph Cotten
John Belushi	Broderick Crawford
William Bendix	Joan Crawford
Jack Benny	Hume Cronyn
Edgar Bergen & Charlie McCarthy	Bing Crosby
Milton Berle	Tom Cruise
Humphrey Bogart	Robert Cummings
Ray Bolger	Jamie Lee Curtis
Marlon Brando	Tony Curtis
Walter Brennan	Dan Dailey
Lloyd Bridges	Bette Davis
Jeff Bridges	Ossie Davis
Louise Brooks	Sammy Davis, Jr.
Sandra Bullock	James Dean
Billie Burke	Olivia De Havilland
	Robert De Niro

Julia Roberts
at the Oscars
in 2004

The Hardy Family's newest!
LOVE FINDS Andy HARDY
with
MICKEY ROONEY
Lewis Stone ★ Judy Garland
and a great M-G-M cast!

Johnny Depp
Kirk Douglas
Michael Douglas
Faye Dunaway
Jimmy Durante
Clint Eastwood
Buddy Ebsen
Nelson Eddy
Douglas Fairbanks
Douglas Fairbanks, Jr.
W.C. Fields
Jane Fonda
Henry Fonda
Joan Fontaiine
Glenn Ford
Harrison Ford
Jodie Foster
Clark Gable
Ava Gardner
John Garfield

Judy Garland
John Gilbert
Jackie Gleason
Betty Grable
Cary Grant
Gene Hackman
Jack Haley
Jean Harlow
William S. Hart
Goldie Hawn
Sterling Hayden
Gabby Hayes
Susan Hayward
Rita Hayworth
Van Heflin
Katherine Hepburn
Charlton Heston
Dustin Hoffman
William Holden
Bob Hope

Edward Everett Horton
Rock Hudson
Holly Hunter
Angelica Huston
John Huston
Burl Ives
Angelina Jolie
Van Johnson
Al Jolson
Danny Kaye
Buster Keaton
Diane Keaton
Gene Kelly
Grace Kelly
Alan Ladd
Bert Lahr
Dorothy Lamour
Burt Lancaster
Jessica Lange
Janet Leigh
Jack Lemmon
Oscar Levant
Jerry Lewis
Harold Lloyd
Carole Lombard
Myrna Loy
Shirley Maclaine
Fred MacMurray
Karl Malden
Fredric March
Dean Martin
Lee Marvin
The Marx Brothers

Raymond Massey
Walter Matthau
Victor Mature
Joel McCrea
Steve McQueen
Burgess Meredith
Ethel Merman
Ray Milland
Ann Miller
Sal Mineo
Robert Mitchum
Tom Mix
Marilyn Monroe
Robert Montgomery
Julianne Moore
Frank Morgan
Patricia Neal
Paul Newman
Jack Nicholson
Edmond O'Brien
Margaret O'Brien

William S. Hart
in
"WHITE OAK"
BY WILLIAM S. HART

A WILLIAM S. HART PRODUCTION
A Paramount Picture

Pat O'Brien	Mickey Rooney
Donald O'Connor	Jane Russell
Al Pacino	Susan Sarandon
Jack Palance	Norma Shearer
Maureen O'Hara	Frank Sinatra
Gwyneth Paltrow	Red Skelton
Gregory Peck	Barbara Stanwyck
Anthony Perkins	James Stewart
Michelle Pfeiffer	Meryl Streep
Slim Pickens	Gloria Swanson
Brad Pitt	Donald Sutherland
Zasu Pitts	Elizabeth Taylor
Sidney Poitier	Robert Taylor
Dick Powell	Shirley Temple
Eleanor Powell	The Three Stooges
William Powell	Spencer Tracy
Tyrone Power	John Travolta
Elvis Presley	Lana Turner
Robert Preston	Rudy Vallee
Anthony Quinn	Jon Voight
George Raft	Denzel Washington
Martha Raye	John Wayne
Ronald Reagan	Sigourney Weaver
Donna Reed	Johnny Weissmuller
Robert Redford	Orson Welles
Lee Remick	Mae West
Burt Reynolds	Richard Widmark
Debbie Reynolds	Cornel Wilde
Julia Roberts	Chill Wills
Paul Robeson	Shelley Winters
Edward G. Robinson	Natalie Wood
Ginger Rogers	Robert Young
Roy Rogers	Rene Zellweger

Tom Hanks

Stay Tuned

Television in America

The evolution of this fascinating medium has taken us from *Dragnet* to *Law and Order*, from *Ted Mack's Original Amateur Hour* to *American Idol*, from the *$64,000 Question* to *Who Wants to be a Millionaire?* and from *I Love Lucy* to *Everybody Loves Raymond*. And where else can you buy an entire set of amazing Ginsu knives or "Patsy Cline's Greatest Hits" at 3:00 a.m.?

441

The wonderful variety of intelligent programming on the Public Broadcasting System (PBS)

442

The endless melodrama of the afternoon soap operas, past and present

General Hospital, One Life to Live, Days of Our Lives, The Guiding Light, *and* The Edge of Night, *to name just a few*

443
America's obsession with
The Weather Channel

444
Ron Popeil and his amazing Chop-o-Matic®,
Veg-o-Matic®, Pocket Fisherman®,
Seal-a-Meal®, and Buttoneer®

445 Tuning into MTV and remarking that you don't recognize any of the new artists...then switching to VH-1 and coming to the same conclusion

446 Curling up on the sofa with your cat and watching *Animal Planet* together

447 Watching old *Lassie* reruns with your dog

448 Making a bowl of popcorn in the microwave and watching old favorites on *Nick at Nite*

449 Taking a "television bus tour" in New York and New Jersey to visit all the hot spots from *Sex And The City*, *Seinfeld*, and *The Sopranos*

450 Discussing Matt Lauer's haircut around the water cooler at the office in the morning

451 The Discovery Channel, The History Channel, and The Learning Channel, where we can actually learn something most of the time

452 The Golf Channel and ESPN all weekend long

453 Watching the Masters Tournament, the World Series, or the NBA playoffs on a giant wide-screen TV

454 Turner Classic Movies on a rainy Saturday afternoon

455 Buying gizmos from QVC and infomercials

456 Watching the Miss America pageant with your mom, your daughter, your sister or your friend

457 Television offers us a glimpse of the evolving American family.

From the simple days of milk & cookie snacks on Leave it to Beaver *to the dysfuntional and extended families like* The Sopranos, *television shows us the many aspects of the American family.*

Happy Days
Ozzie & Harriet
The Wonder Years
The Waltons
Little House On The Prairie
Everybody Loves Raymond

The Cosby Show
Roseanne
The Simpsons

458 There's always a chance to win big bucks on the American game show.

Where else can you combine your mental acumen and your capacity to yell, shriek, and jump up and down at the same time?

Jeopardy
Wheel of Fortune
Queen For A Day
To Tell the Truth
Password
Hollywood Squares
What's My Line?
The $64,000 Question
The Newlywed Game

459 We enjoy watching someone else's problems on shows about the American legal system.

Where most of our citizens learned they have the right to remain silent...

LA Law
Perry Mason
The Practice
Court TV

Law & Order
Judd for the Defense
Matlock

460 There's nothing better than a good car chase on American cop shows.

The battle between good and evil has played itself out since the early days of television.

Dragnet
The Untouchables
NYPD Blue
Hawaii Five-O

Hill Street Blues
Starsky and Hutch
Cagney and Lacey
Miami Vice

461 We celebrate our frontier heritage with American westerns.

The good guys wore white hats and protected the town from gunslingers and horse thieves. The western taught America right from wrong, and how to play poker.

Gunsmoke
Rawhide
Bonanza
Death Valley Days

The Rifleman
Have Gun Will Travel
Maverick
The Big Valley

462
The Ed Sullivan Show

The Beetles made their
American TV debut on
February 9, 1964

463 American sitcoms have kept the world laughing since George Burns and Gracie Allen.

Couch potatoes across the country can sit and watch OTHER people get in and out of messy and sometimes hilarious situations...

I Love Lucy

The Burns and Allen Show

The Dick Van Dyke Show

Green Acres

All in the Family

The Beverly Hillbillies

Fraiser

Cheers

Seinfeld

Mash

Friends

464 The endless variety of variety shows

American television found a niche for jugglers, ventriloquists, opera singing parrots, rockstars, gymnasts, and roller skating poodles in tutus.

Ed Sullivan

Sonny and Cher

The Carol Burnett Show

Rowan and Martin's Laugh-In

Ted Mack's Original Amateur Hour

The Jackie Gleason Show
  (with the June Taylor Dancers)

465
The wonderful Jack Paar

466
The Tonight Show

467 From the Today Show to
The Tonight Show, we love
American's talk shows.
They interview everyone from starlets
to princesses and keep us up late
wondering what will happen next.

Jack Paar
The Tonight Show
Late Show with David Letterman
Merv Griffin
The Mike Douglas Show
Conan O'Brien
Larry King
Oprah Winfrey
Phil Donahue

468 Learning can be fun with
American children's television
Generations of children have grown up
watching some great American TV!

Captain Kangaroo
Sesame Street
Rocky & Bullwinkle
The Howdy Doody Show
The Mickey Mouse Club
SpongeBob SquarePants
Mr. Roger's Neighborhood

Ten American Baseball Legends

469 Baseball Hall of Famer Ty Cobb

The "Georgia Peach" played an aggressive, intimidating, hustling style of baseball for 22 years with Detroit (and a couple with Philadelphia) that earned him the honor of being the first man elected to baseball's Hall of Fame. His abrasive personality won him few friends but he hit over .300 in 22 of the 24 years and is regarded as one of baseball's all-time best.

470 Ageless Satchel Paige

"Satchel" was one of the Negro Leagues' finest baseball pitchers in the '20s and '30s, dominating hitters in his many appearances. After he became a major-leaguer, he never divulged his correct age but demonstrated why he was ageless when he pitched three scoreless innings for the Kansas City Athletics in 1965 at the approximate age of 59. He was elected to baseball's Hall of Fame in 1971.

471 Babe Ruth

He earned his nicknames The Babe, Sultan of Swat, and The Great Bambino while teamed with fellow Yankee, Lou Gehrig, as they terrorized baseball's American League with their power hitting. He pitched well

too: 70 wins and 40 losses with Boston. But The Babe will always be remembered and revered for his ability to hit 'em out of the park.*

472 Casey Stengel

He wasn't too bad when he played in baseball's major leagues for 12 years, but he became renowned for his success as a manager for the Dodgers, the Braves, the Yankees, and the Mets. His Yankees won 7 world titles, 10 pennants, and a lot of respect in a remarkable 12-year run. He is also fondly remembered for his unique gift of gab as well as his induction into baseball's Hall of Fame.

473 Lou Gehrig

He was called the Iron Man because he played in 2,130 consecutive baseball games for the New York Yankees. And he played hard: batted over .300 for 12 years in a row, won the American League home run title three times, and was the RBI leader five times. Gehrig's baseball career ended when ALS (Amytrophic Lateral Sclerosis), afterwards known as Lou Gehrig's disease, struck him down. His fans, and America in general, considered themselves lucky to have known such a man. His life, and his poignant farewell speech, were captured in the film The Pride of the Yankees, starring Gary Cooper.

474 Ted Williams

He wore number 9 and he was one of baseball's greatest hitters, winning six American League hitting championships. His lifetime batting average was .314, he was chosen for 17 All Star games, and he hit 521 home runs, even though he was away from baseball for five seasons serving America as a marine pilot during World War ll. A bonafide hero too. The Fenway Park fans and the world mourned when we lost him July 5, 2002.

475 Cal Ripken Jr.

In 1995 at his home field in Baltimore, Cal broke Lou Gehrig's amazing record by playing in 2,131 consecutive baseball games. He didn't stop there. It was three years before he decided to take a day off after playing in 501 more games without a break. He amassed many of baseball's highest honors such as two-time American League Most Valuable Player and participant in 17 straight All Star games. He has fans all over America.

476 Jackie Robinson

He had superb athletic skills that propelled him into a historical position in America when he became the first black baseball player in the major leagues. He couldn't be ignored or dismissed, for he was a terror on the base paths, helping the Brooklyn Dodgers win six pennants in 10 seasons. He became a symbol of what was possible for black people in America.

477 Joe DiMaggio

"Joltin' Joe" may have set a baseball record that will stand for all time: his 56-consecutive game hitting streak in 1941. His hitting ability (he won two batting championships and three Most Valuable Player awards), his graceful athleticism as he ran the bases, and his steadiness in the field helped the New York Yankees to many championships. He may have been the best all-round baseball player ever.

478 Hank Aaron

Hammerin' Hank was the last baseball player to come to the major leagues from the Negro Leagues, but perhaps one of the best. He eclipsed "the Babe's" home run record of 755, set 12 other baseball records over his 23 year career, and appeared in 24 All-Star games.

LEGENDS OF AMERICAN SPORTS

They entertain, inspire and amaze us with their ability to run, jump, tackle, pass, putt, and soar through the air. These heroes of American sports show us what we could become with talent, determination, and the will to be the best.

479 Vince Lombardi

He led the Green Bay Packers to five National Football League championships and victories in the first two Super Bowls in the '60s with his unrelenting style of coaching. His famous quote, "If winning isn't everything, why do they keep score?" exemplifies the philosophy he instilled in his players who believed in him. His winning percentage of .740 made him the most revered NFL coach.

480 Johnny Unitas

His determination, football acumen, and passing abilities propelled him to NFL stardom over his eighteen-year career. His National Football League record elevates him to the elite level as one of football's greatest quarterbacks. When he retired, he had passed for over 40,000 yards, set 22 records, led the Baltimore Colts to three NFL championships, and been in 10 Pro Bowls. He left us too soon at age 69.

481 Walter Payton

The football fans of Chicago love "Da Bears" and adored "Sweetness" especially when he accelerated away from the line for another touchdown. He gave his fans 12 wonderful years of excitement. When he retired, he was the all-time leader in running and combined net yards. His versatility showed when he caught or passed the ball. We lost him to cancer too soon—in 1999.

482 Earvin "Magic" Johnson

Magic's broad smile as he dished off a quick and wondrous no-look pass gave you an idea of how much he loved the game of basketball and how good he was. He made things happen, he generated excitement, and he won on the court from his days in Lansing at Michigan State University to the 13 years he spent with the L.A. Lakers.

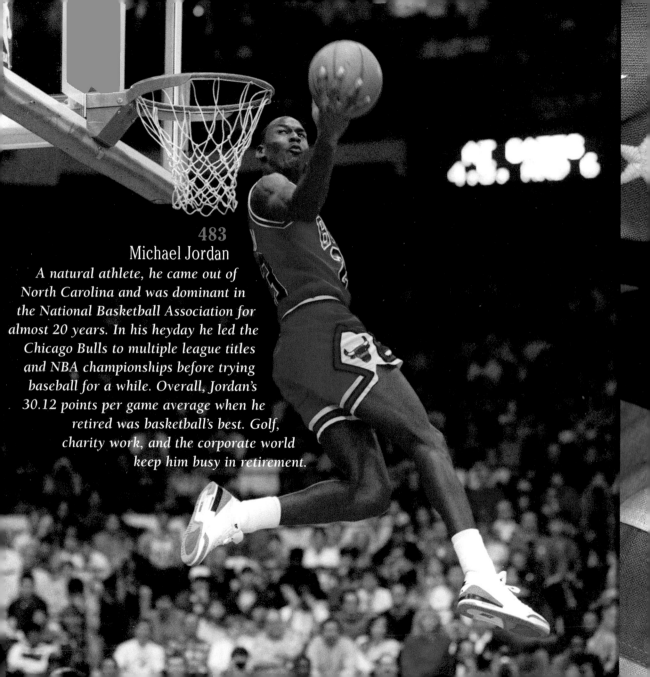

483
Michael Jordan

*A natural athlete, he came out of
North Carolina and was dominant in
the National Basketball Association for
almost 20 years. In his heyday he led the
Chicago Bulls to multiple league titles
and NBA championships before trying
baseball for a while. Overall, Jordan's
30.12 points per game average when he
retired was basketball's best. Golf,
charity work, and the corporate world
keep him busy in retirement.*

Dale Earnhardt and Dale
Earnhardt Jr., February, 2000

484 Dale Earnhardt

The "Intimidator" knew he wanted to be the best in motor sports, and he became a legend. He raced to the lead in stock cars on short tracks and then in NASCAR events, eventually winning the Daytona 500 in 1998 after 20 tries. He died when he crashed his Chevy number 3 at the Daytona 500 in 2001, precipitating an outpouring of grief from his adoring American fans.

485 A. J. Foyt

When he retired in 1993, he was the only racecar driver who won the Indianapolis 500, the Daytona 500, and the 24 Hours of Le Mans. He began his racing career in midgets then showed his versatility by racing on dirt tracks, oval speedways, and road courses. Along the way, among many triumphs on the track, he won seven national driving championships to prove that he was one of the greatest American racecar drivers.

486 Richard Petty

Over the course of 32 years and multiple NASCAR Winston Cup courses, "The King" amassed a whopping 200 race victories. He had watched his daddy, Lee, win three Grand National (now Winston Cup) championships and caught the fever. When his career ended in 1992, The King had won the prestigious Daytona 500 seven times, accumulated 27 race victories in just one year, and won seven Winston Cup Championships overall.

487 The Brown Bomber, Joe Lewis

The Brown Bomber, as he was affectionately known, came out of Detroit and dominated the heavyweight boxing world during the '30s and the '40s, holding the heavyweight championship for twelve straight years. In 1938 he represented America and the world when he stunned Hitler's Nazi propaganda machine by knocking out German boxer Max Schmeling in the first round of a bitter rematch, proving Aryans were not the supreme people.

488 Muhammad Ali (Cassius Clay)

"The Greatest" never lost his desire and determination to be the best. Whether it was in the boxing ring where his strategies, power, and skills won fame, or in the public arena where he spoke out about his beliefs and influenced generations of Americans in the '60s and '70s. During the divisive times when racial equality and the Vietnam War were America's issues, Ali's "never surrender" attitude never wavered.

489 Jesse Owens

In elementary school they knew he had the raw talent to excel in track and field. And did he ever, on through high school, college, and eventually the Olympic Games. He excelled even though he had to hurdle the high barriers set by segregation in American in the '30s. He persevered and set many world track and field records. Jesse will be remembered best for spoiling Hitler's plans to prove that the Nazi "Aryan" race was superior in the 1936 Olympic Games. In the end, Jesse won four gold medals, the respect of the German people, and the hearts of the world.

490 Peggy Fleming

After her coach was killed with the rest of the U.S. Olympic figure skating team in a tragic air crash in 1961, 13-year old Peggy Fleming was determined to continue her promising figure skating career. Her graceful style dominated the skating World Championships for three years before she won the hearts of the American public and the U.S. team's only gold medal at the 1966 winter Olympic. Her recent courageous fight with breast cancer proves she continues to be a champion.

491 Billie Jean King

In the late '60s and '70s, she used her athletic abilities to help wake America to the idea that women's rights and equality of the sexes were major issues. Billie Jean lobbied for female athletes to earn as much money as men as she won major tennis championships: 20 times at Wimbledon and 13 U. S. Opens. In 1973, a huge American audience watched her wreck Bobby Riggs in a "Battle of the Sexes" match that generated an enormous amount of hoopla and debate. When it was over, U.S. women had a special heroine who did not back down and carried a big tennis racquet.

492 Arthur Ashe

His thin frame belied his athletic talent. When he showed promise at tennis in his hometown of Richmond, Virginia, he gained a mentor in Dr. Walter Johnson who had coached Althea Gibson. Ten years later, Arthur became the first African-American to be named to the U.S. Davis Cup team. He won three Grand Slams and was the only black man to win the U.S. Open and Wimbledon. A heart condition cut short his tennis career, but he continued to work for human rights until he died at the age of 49.

493

Jackie Joyner-Kersee

When she was born, Jackie was named for the first lady of America, Jackie Kennedy, because her parents felt she would be special. That specialty was athletics. She was a high school All-American in basketball and track before heading to UCLA for four years of record-breaking performances in track and field. Winning became her habit in the Good Will, Pan-American, and finally the Olympic Games. Her apex came when she became the first athlete of either sex to win multi-event medals in three separate Olympics.

Jackie Joyner-Kersee competes in the long jump finals of the U.S. Olympics Track and Field Trials, July, 2000.

494 Chris Evert

Chris was the daughter of tennis pro Jimmie Evert, who may have taught her the wicked two-handed backhand that gave her a very steady and reliable base-line game. It was hard to hit one past her. That and her unflappability during her 18-year career resulted in 157 tournament wins and almost nine million dollars in earnings once she turned professional.

495 Bobby Jones

Better known as Bobby Jones, Robert Tyre Jones Jr., electrified millions of adoring fans when he achieved the impossible feat of capturing all four major golf championships in 1930. Jones retired from competitive golf at age 28, shortly after his "Grand Slam" triumph, but remains one of the truly inspirational American sports legends. Jones also founded the Augusta National Golf Club and the Masters Golf Tournament.

496 Babe Didrikson Zaharias

Voted Best Woman Athlete of the Millennium. Mildred began playing base-ball as a youngster in Texas where she got her nickname, Babe, because some thought she could hit the ball like Babe Ruth. She excelled in many sports, winning two gold medals in track at the 1932 Los Angeles Olympic Games. Babe became so good at golf that she was invited to play in a Professional Golf Association event against men—and made the cut. She was among the founders of the LPGA in 1953.

497 Tiger Woods

Eldrick (Tiger) Woods was just 21 years old when he burst onto the international golf scene with a spectacular, 12-shot victory at the 1997 Masters Tournament. After capturing his second Masters in 2001, he also became the first golfer ever to hold all four professional championship titles at once. With his unique combination of good looks, athletic talent and absolute dedication to the game, he sets the standard for sports excellence.

498 Wilma Rudolph

Wilma, who was the 20th of 22 siblings, suffered many ills as a youngster including polio that gave her a bad leg. Her resolution to walk normally drove her to become involved in basketball and track, and she soon began to win. At 16, she won her first Olympic medal—a bronze. That seemed to increase her desire and persistence to win even more. In Rome she became the first American woman ever to win three gold medals. She was only 54 when she died, but her contribution to help overcome America's practice of segregation is a legacy.

499
Ben Hogan

He was called The Hawk and known for his intense determination, obsessive practice regimen, and acute desire to win every golf tournament he entered. In 1949 those characteristics helped Ben battle back to glory after being severely injured in a car accident. The man from Texas astonished the golf world when he won the intensely competitive U.S. Open the very next year. He is third on the all-time win list with 63 tour victories, and his book on the fundamentals of golf is still a best seller.

Ben Hogan at the Los Angeles Open on January 5, 1950, just 11 months after his near-fatal car acident.

143

AMERICAN PASTIMES
HANGING OUT AND OTHER
THINGS TO DO

We love our free time and fill it up with an endless
variety of interesting activities.

500
Getting up early to go birdwatching

501
The profund satisfaction of gardening

502
Going to the gym to prepare for swimsuit season

503
Lounging in a bubblebath with the new issue
of the *National Enquirer*

504
Planning a Sunday brunch in the city with friends

505
Taking your dog on a big hike in the country

506
Knitting, quilting, embroidering

507
Wasting time on the Internet looking for old
boyfriends from long ago

508
Shopping for nothing in particular

509
Hanging out in your room prac-
ticing "Smoke on the Water"
on your electric guitar and
dreaming of life as a rock star

510
Learning to fly fish,
paddle a canoe, identify four
kinds of pine trees, and
build a good campfire

511
Receiving packages from
home filled with
Rice Krispies squares,
clean underwear,
and love

512
Waking up early to go on a
hike through a forest
filled with wonders

513
Staying up late to watch
for shooting stars

514
Going to sleep-away
summer camp
in a faraway north woods
wilderness by a lake

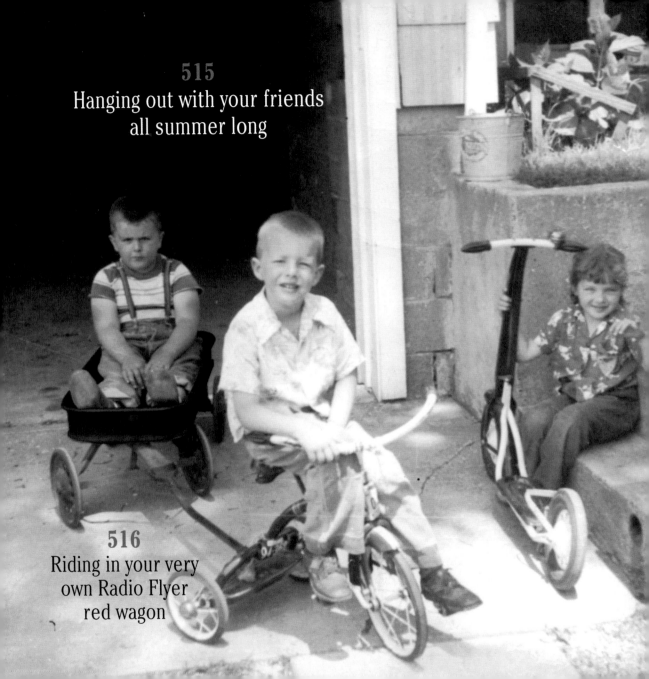

515
Hanging out with your friends
all summer long

516
Riding in your very
own Radio Flyer
red wagon

517
After-school basketball, baseball, tennis, lacrosse, football, and soccer practice

518
Going to the mall with your friends and walking around looking for your other friends

519
Talking on the phone with your best friend about music and shoes and parents and the cute new boy in school

520
Sitting on the front stoop of the apartment building and watching the world go by

521
A weekend fishing trip with your dad where you learn to catch perch, make scrambled eggs, and get to hear stories about when he was a little kid

522
Swimming, diving, waterskiing, parasailing,
surfing, boating, canoeing, and lounging
in beach chairs with a cold drink

523

Mall walking

524
Poker nights

525
Book clubs

526
Organizing a girl's night out

527
Going to dinner and a movie

528
Spending a weekend at the ashram for a
yoga and meditation retreat

529
Taking an evening class in creative writing,
art history, French or Feng Shui

530
Refining your golf game
on a winter afternoon

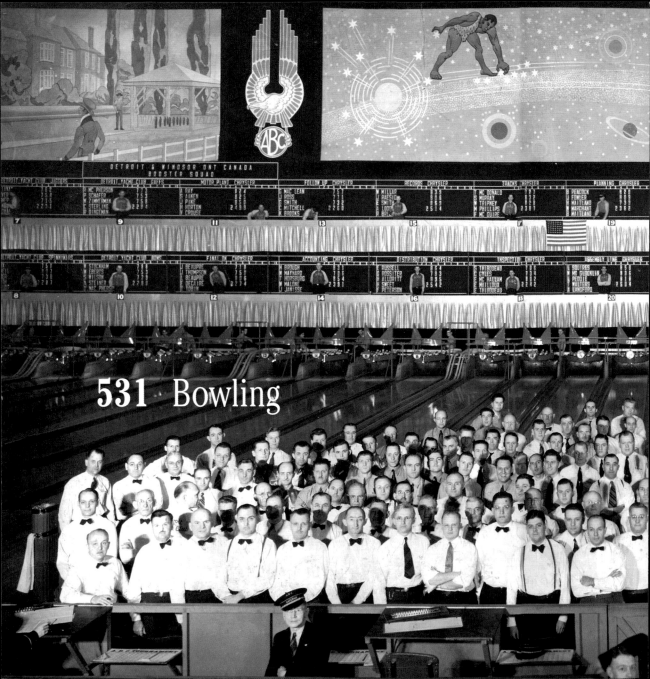

531 Bowling

The American Bowling Congress,
Detroit, Michigan, 1940

From Sea to Shining Sea

Somewhere in the back of every American's mind, and in the minds of a lot of people around the world, lies the dream of the ultimate American road trip. With vast, dramatic landscapes, 12,500 miles of coastline, and every possible type of climate and vegetation, the map of the United States is an open invitation to adventure. Add America's fascinating mix of cultures and interests, and our itinerary abounds with more beautiful scenery, interesting landmarks and roadside oddities than one can explore in a lifetime!

The Oregon Coast at sunset

OUR NATIONAL PARKS

Our national parks are treasures we share and preserve for future generations.
Nowhere else can we experience the diversity of the American landscape, the incredible
beauty and grandeur of the earth, and the power of reconnecting with nature.

532 Acadia National Park (Maine)
This park includes mountains, woodlands, and lakes on a group of islands dotted along the coast of Maine. Acadia was the first national park established east of the Mississippi.

533 Badlands National Park (South Dakota)
Founded in 1939 as a national monument, Badlands National Park was designated a national park in 1978. The park's 244,000 acres include incredible pinnacles, buttes, and spires, with fossil beds dating back 23 million years. Badlands National Park includes the largest protected mixed grass prairie in the U.S. This is the park to visit if you want to see a black-footed ferret!

534 Bryce Canyon National Park (Utah)
Formed by erosion due to wind, rain, and ice, Bryce displays an incredible variety of sharp, rust-red spires of limestone, called "hoodoos." Bryce became a national park in 1924.

535 Saguaro National Park (Arizona)
This desert park is home to the most recognizable cactus in the world, the majestic saguaro. A saguaro cactus typically lives for 150 years and reaches a height of 50 feet.

536 Carlsbad Caverns National Park
(New Mexico) *Carlsbad Caverns boasts one of the world's largest underground chambers and countless formations. The park has over 100 other limestone caves including Lechuguilla Cave, the deepest limestone cave in America.*

537 Petrified Forest National Park (Arizona)
This park contains the world's largest and most colorful collection of petrified wood. Also within the park are the multi-hued badlands known as the Painted Desert and deposits containing 225 million-year-old fossils.

538 Denali National Park and Preserve
(Alaska) *Covering more than six million acres, Denali is home to spectacular mountains, vast glaciers and 20,320-foot high Mount McKinley, North America's highest elevation.*

539
Death Valley National Park (California)

The average temperature in summer is well over 100 degrees with an annual rainfall of less than two inches, making it one of the hottest and driest places anywhere on Earth. Death Valley is also the lowest spot in the Western Hemisphere—282 feet below sea level.

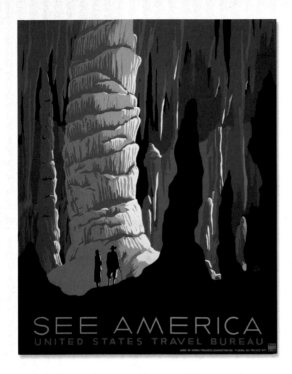

SEE AMERICA
UNITED STATES TRAVEL BUREAU

540 Glen Canyon National Recreation Area (Arizona and Utah)

This National Recreation Area offers unparalleled water and back country recreation extending for hundreds of miles from Lees Ferry, Arizona, to the Orange Cliffs of Southern Utah. The controversy caused by the construction of the Glen Canyon Dam that created Lake Powell fueled the modern day environmental movement.

541 Everglades National Park (Florida)

North America's only subtropical preserve, the park occupies the southern tip of Florida and most of Florida Bay. It includes a variety of environments from swamps to pinelands and is home to a great variety of animal life. Here visitors can see large wading birds such as the roseate spoonbill. Only in the Everglades do crocodiles and alligators live side by side.

542 Great Smoky Mountains National Park

(Tennessee and North Carolina) *The park is one of the largest protected areas in the eastern U.S. Made up of ridge after ridge of seemingly endless forest straddling two states, it is a hiker's paradise with over 800 miles of trails.*

543 Hawaii Volcanoes National Park (Hawaii)

All of the islands making up Hawaii were created by 70 million years of volcanic activity. This park, created in 1916, includes Mauna Loa the world's most massive volcano, towering 13,677 feet above the sea, and Kilauea, the most active volcano anywhere.

544 Mammoth Cave National Park (Kentucky)

Mammoth Cave is part of a cave system extending 360 miles, the longest known cave system in the world. In addition to protecting the cave system, the park was created to preserve the scenic Green and Nolin River valleys plus a section of south central Kentucky.

THE NATIONAL PARKS
PRESERVE WILD LIFE

MADE BY WORKS PROGRESS ADMINISTRATION · FEDERAL ART PROJECT NYC

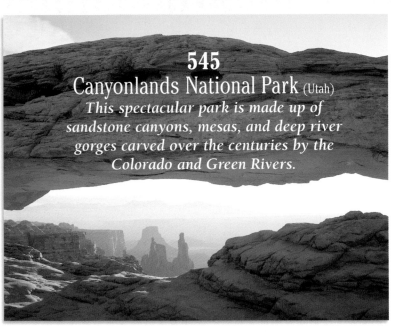

545
Canyonlands National Park (Utah)
This spectacular park is made up of sandstone canyons, mesas, and deep river gorges carved over the centuries by the Colorado and Green Rivers.

546 **Mount Rainier National Park** (Washington)

Established in 1899, 97% of the park's nearly one-quarter million acres is designated wilderness. The active volcano, Mount Rainier, reaches a height of 14,410 feet and is covered by 35 square miles of snow and ice.

547
Grand Canyon National Park (Arizona and Utah)

It took the Colorado River hundreds of centuries to carve this deep chasm.
Designated a national monument in 1908, it achieved park status in 1919.
No photograph can do justice to the scale and beauty of the Grand Canyon.
Visitors can enjoy panoramas of many miles from the rim, walk up and down
its rocky trails, or raft the Colorado River through the bottom of canyons.

548
Arches National Park (Utah)

This park boasts the greatest concentration of natural arches in the world, over 2,000. Arches is a geologic treasure because of its many unusual landforms.

SEE AMERICA
UNITED STATES TRAVEL BUREAU

549 Redwood National and Sta Parks (California) *Three state parks and the National Park Service are cooperating to preserve redwood forests. The parks contain 45 percent of California's old-growth redwoc forest. These trees can live for 2000 years and reach a height of over 360 feet.*

550 Sequoia & Kings Canyon National Parks (California) *The giant sequoia is the world largest tree. The oldest is 3200 years old! Some of the largest individual trees were named fo Civil War generals. The tree named for General Sherman i nearly 275 feet tall.*

551 Yellowstone National Park
(Idaho, Montana, and Wyoming)
Much of the park is occupied by a vast crater thirty miles wide and forty-five miles long, which was created about 640,000 years ago by a massive volcanic explosion. The cauldrons of bubbling mud and roaring geysers, such as Old Faithful, are proof of continuous volcanic activity beneath the park.

552 Zion National Park (Utah)
The park's 229 square miles contain not only dramatic landscapes of sculptured canyons and soaring cliffs, but also great plant and animal diversity resulting from the intersection of three distinct climatic zones within Zion.

greetings from...
YOSEMITE
NATIONAL PARK

553
Yosemite National Park
(California)
Famous for its incredible scenery, Yosemite is one of the most visited parks. The best-known location within the park is the Yosemite Valley with its dramatic cliffs and waterfalls.

America's Most Beautiful Roads

The most beautiful road in America is **U.S. 212**, which leaves Red Lodge, climbs to Beartooth Pass at 11,000 feet, and drops down into the northeast entrance of Yellowstone Park. Don't try it in winter . . . U.S. 212 spends the winter under many feet of snow. When the road opens, usually in May, the folks in Cooke City set up a booth to give the first day's intrepid motorists free drinks on the way through. It's that kind of highway. There will still be snow up there in August, but it's America's most beautiful road.

Second is **California Route 1** along the coast from Morro Bay to Monterey. That's the road William Randolph Hearst built his castle on. (He'd have built his castle on the Red Lodge-Cooke City highway if he'd known about it.)

Third is the **Going to the Sun Highway** across Glacier Park. Fourth is **U.S. 550** in Colorado, from Montrose to Durango. Fifth is **Hawaii Route 56** from Lihue to Haena on the island of Kauai, but where the island really gets pretty is where the road ends and you have to start walking.

The sixth most beautiful road in America is the **Blue Ridge Parkway** in the spring. Seventh is **Vermont Route 100** in the fall. Eighth is a road chosen for what's on it, **U.S. 61,** through Vicksburg and Natchez to New Orleans. Ninth is chosen for what's not on it, **North Carolina Route 12,** down the Outer Banks from Nags Head to Hatteras and by ferry to Ocracoke Island. Those are America's most beautiful roads. Anybody want to argue?

Charles Kuralt
Dateline America

554
A drive up the California coast, along the Pacific Ocean, and through the Redwood forests

UNITED · STATES · TRAVEL · BU
DEPARTMENT OF THE INTERIOR

DESTINATIONS, DRIVES, & DETOURS
DISCOVERING AMERICA

Americans are fond of taking to the road,
and every state offers new adventures, whether
famous destinations or hidden gems.

*A 9.5 mile drive along the
Atlantic shores offering views
of Newport's incredible
mansions.*

~ 168 ~

Alaska's Seward Highway

582

The fifty great states that make up the United States of America

Alabama: The Yellowhammer State
Alaska: The Last Frontier
Arizona: The Grand Canyon State
Arkansas: The Natural State
California: The Golden State
Colorado: The Centennial State
Connecticut: The Constitution State
Delaware: The First State
Florida: The Sunshine State
Georgia: The Peach State
Hawaii: The Aloha State
Idaho: The Gem State
Illinois: The Prairie State
Indiana: The Hoosier State
Iowa: The Hawkeye State
Kansas: The Sunflower State
Kentucky: The Bluegrass State
Louisiana: The Pelican State
Maine: The Pine Tree State
Maryland: The Old Line State
Massachusetts: The Bay State
Michigan: The Wolverine State
Minnesota: The Land of 10,000 Lakes
Mississippi: The Magnolia State
Missouri: The Show Me State
Montana: The Treasure State
Nebraska: The Cornhusker State
Nevada: The Silver State

New Hampshire: The Granite State
New Jersey: The Garden State
New Mexico: Land of Enchantment
New York: The Empire State
North Carolina: The Old North State
North Dakota: The Peace Garden State
Ohio: The Buckeye State
Oklahoma: The Sooner State
Oregon: The Beaver State
Pennsylvania: The Keystone State
Rhode Island: The Ocean State
South Carolina: The Palmetto State
South Dakota: The Mount Rushmore State
Tennessee: The Volunteer State
Texas: The Lone Star State
Utah: The Beehive State
Vermont: The Green Mountain State
Virginia: The Old Dominion State
Washington: The Evergreen State
West Virginia: The Mountain State
Wisconsin: The Badger State
Wyoming: The Equality State

Greetings from MISSISSIPPI

Greetings from NEVADA — MISSOURI — "SEEIN'S BELIEVIN'"

Souvenir from MONTANA

Greetings from NEW JERSEY

GREETINGS FROM NEW MEXICO — THE SUNSHINE STATE

GREETINGS From NEW YORK

Greetings from OKLAHOMA

Greetings From OREGON

Greetings from PENNSYLVANIA

Greetings from TENNESSEE

Greetings from TEXAS

Greetings from UTAH

Greetings FROM WEST VIRGINIA

Greetings from WISCONSIN

Greetings from WYOMING

HISTORIC ROUTE 66

MOTEL

DIRECT DIAL PHONES
QUEEN BEDS
CABLE T.V.   H.B.O.
LARGE FAMILY ROOMS

VACANCY

Roadkill
66 CAFE
STEAK HOUSE

STEAKS   BURGERS
ALL Y OU CA NEAT
SALA D BA R
OPE N 11AM

Route 66

John Steinbeck called it "the mother road, the road of flight." Some, like the Okies, knew it as the "glory road." Because it went through the center of so many towns, it became the "Main Street of America."

Route 66 is Steinbeck and Will Rogers and Woody Guthrie and Merle Haggard and Dorothea Lange and Mickey Mantle and Jack Kerouac. It's thousands of waitresses, service station attendants, fry cooks, truckers, grease monkeys, hustlers, state cops, wrecker drivers, and motel clerks. Route 66 is a soldier thumbing home for Christmas; an Okie family still looking for a better life. It's a station wagon filled with kids wanting to know how far it is to Disneyland; a wailing ambulance fleeing a wreck on some lonely curve. It's yesterday, today, and tomorrow. Truly a road of phantoms and dreams, 66 is the romance of traveling the open highway.

The highway has been a mirror held up to the nation. Route 66 put Americans in touch with other Americans through its necklace of neon lights, Burma shave signs, curio shops, motor courts, garages, and diners and cafés with big-boned waitresses. Waitresses who served up burgers, plate lunches, and homemade pie. Waitresses with coffeepots welded to their fists. Waitresses with handkerchief corsages pinned on their bosoms. Waitresses, like Steinbeck's Mae, who called everybody "honey," winked at the kids, and yelled at the cook.

… A thread looping together a giant patchwork of Americana, this fabled road represents much more than just another American highway. Route 66 means motion and excitement. It's the mythology of the open road. Migrants traveled its length; so did desperadoes and vacationers. Few highways provoke such an overwhelming response. When people think of Route 66, they picture a road to adventure.

Michael Wallis,
Route 66, The Mother Road

584

Las Vegas!

Some Things to Do in Las Vegas Besides Gamble

Visit the hotels and casinos just to see the amazing architecture.

Take a drive to Hoover Dam or the Red Rock Canyon area and walk through the Valley of Fire.

Dine at the all-you-can-eat buffets.

Hang by the pool.

Go to the top of the Stratosphere Tower for cocktails and a fabulous nighttime view.

Visit the Eiffel Tower, the Statue of Liberty and take a ride in a gondola all in the same day.

Shop in the Forum Shops at Caesar's Palace and watch the weather change indoors.

Visit the Elvis-a-Rama Museum, the Liberace Museum, and the art gallery at Bellagio.

Get married at the Little White Wedding Chapel (open 24/7)!

I'M FROM IDIOTVILLE
AMERICA'S UNUSUAL TOWN NAMES

While Pennsylvania is famous for Intercourse and Mississippi is proud of its Hot Coffee,
nothing can beat Delightful, Ohio and Nice, California. Many American towns have colorful names
with curious histories. Take a trip to Mars, send a postcard from
Hell, and take a drive through Kansas. You might pass Gas.

585 Truth or Consequences,
    New Mexico

586 Embarrass, Illinois

587 Gas, Kansas

588 Intercourse, Pennsylvania
    and Alabama

589 Monkey's Eyebrow, Kentucky

590 Knockemstiff, Ohio

591 Hell, Michigan

592 Holy Moses, Colorado

593 Accident, Maryland

594 Hot Coffee, Mississippi

595 Pickles Gap, Arkansas

596 Butt's Corner, New York

597 Bow Legs, Oklahoma

598 Boogertown, Ohio

599 Satan's Kingdom, Vermont

600 Purgatory, Maine

601 Peculiar, Missouri

To Lake *Aghmoogenegamook*,
All in the State of Maine,
A man from *Wittequergaugaum* came
One evening in the rain.

R.H. Newell, *The American Traveler*, 1863

602 Boring, Oregon
603 Dull, Ohio
604 Odd, West Virginia
605 Mars, Pennsylvania
606 Delightful, Ohio
607 Happy, Texas
608 Nice, California
609 Difficult, Tennessee
610 Toad Suck, Arkansas

611 Nothing, Arizona
612 Nameless, Texas
613 Bear Butte, South Dakota
614 Bottom, North Carolina
615 Why, Arizona
616 Two Egg, Florida
617 Chicken, Alaska
618 Looneyville, Texas
619 Idiotville, Oregon

" ... a chorus of sweet and

"There is no part of the world," said Robert Louis Stevenson, "where nomenclature is so rich, poetical, humorous and picturesque as the United States of America. All times, races and languages have brought their contribution. **Pekin** is in the same State with **Euclid**, with **Bellfontaine**, and with **Sandusky**. The names of the States themselves form a chorus of sweet and most romantic vocables: **Delaware, Ohio, Indiana, Florida, Dakota, Iowa, Wyoming, Minnesota, and the Carolinas:** there are few poems with a nobler music for the ear: a songful, tuneful land."

most romantic vocables..."

The map of the country is besprinkled with place-names
from at least half a hundred languages, living and dead, and
among them one finds examples of the most daring and
charming fancy. There are Spanish, French, and Indian names
as melodious and charming as running water; there are
names out of the histories and mythologies of all the great
races of man; there are names grotesque and names almost
sublime. "***Mississippi***!" rhapsodized Walt Whitman; "the
word winds with chutes—it rolls a stream three thousand
miles long . . . ***Monongahela***! it rolls with venison richness
upon the palate."

H.L. Mencken,
The American Language, 1937

620
Emerald City

Seattle, Washington

FROM BEANTOWN TO TINSELTOWN

AMERICA'S BIG CITY NICKNAMES

Cities often get their nicknames for obvious reasons. Oil City, Rubber City, and Sin City all make sense. But Paris of the Midwest?

621 **rubber city**: *Akron, Ohio*

622 The Athens of the South: *Atlanta, Georgia*

623 *The Windy City*: *Chicago, Illinois*

624 **Big D**: *Dallas, Texas*

625 *The Big Easy*: *New Orleans, Louisiana*

626 **The Big Apple**: *New York, New York*

627 **The Mile High City**: *Denver, Colorado*

628 Motor City, Motown, Paris of the Midwest: *Detroit, Michigan*

629 COW TOWN: *Fort Worth, Texas*

630 Tinseltown: *Hollywood, California*

631 **Oil City**: *Houston, Texas*

632 **Sin City**, Lost Wages: *Las Vegas, Nevada*

633 The Twin Cities: *Minneapolis and St. Paul, Minnesota*

634 **Music City USA**: *Nashville, Tennessee*

635 The City of Brotherly Love: *Philadelphia, Pennsylvania*

636 **Steel City**: *Pittsburgh, Pennsylvania*

637 GATEWAY TO THE WEST: *St. Louis, Missouri*

638 **beantown**: *Boston, Massachusetts*

639 The GIBRALTAR OF AMERICA: *Vicksburg, Mississippi*

640 *City of Angels*: *Los Angeles, California*

Ice Cream, Barbed Wire and Prunes

America's Self-Proclaimed World Capitals

Local pride can lead to world domination, and these towns prove it.

641 **Fire Hydrant Capital of the World:** *Albertville, Alabama*

642 **Rodeo Capital of the World:** *Cody, Wyoming*

643 **Truck Capital of the World:** *Allentown, Pennsylvania*

644 **Bourbon Capital of the World:** *Bardstown, Kentucky*

645 **Cow Chip Throwing Capital of the World:** *Beaver, Oklahoma*

646 **Potato Capital of the World:** *Blackfoot, Idaho*

647 **Peanut Capital of the World:** *Blakely, Georgia*

648 **Artichoke Capital of the World:** *Castroville, California*

649 **Watermelon Capital of the World:** *Cordele, Georgia*

650 **Spinach Capital of the World:** *Crystal City, Texas (in contention with Alma, Arkansas)*

651 **Carpet Capital of the World:** *Dalton, Georgia*

652 **Jackalope Capital of the World:** *Douglas, Wyoming*

653 **Cherry Pit Spitting Capital of the World:** *Eau Claire, Michigan*

654 **Cucumber Capital of the World:** *Webster, Florida*

655 **RV Capital of the World:** *Elkhart, Indiana*

656 **Prune Capital of the World:** *Yuba City, California*

The Kind We Raise in Our State.

657 Official Sock Capital of the World: *Fort Payne, Alabama*

658 Golf Capital of the World: *Myrtle Beach, South Carolina*

659 Garlic Capital of the World: *Gilroy, California*

660 Jambalaya Capital of the World: *Gonzales, Louisiana*

661 Chile Capital of the World: *Hatch, New Mexico*

662 Asparagus Capitals of the World: *Stockton, California; Isleton, California*

663 Barbed Wire Capital of the World: *La Crosse, Kansas*

664 Ice Cream Capital of the World: *Le Mars, Iowa*

665 Popcorn Capitals of the World: *Marion, Ohio; Sac County, Iowa*

666 Honeymoon Capital of the World: *Niagara Falls, New York*

667 Denture Capital of the World: *Florence, South Carolina*

668 Celery Capital of the World: *Chula Vista, California*

669 Hubcap Capital of the World: *Pearsonville, California*

670 Weather Capital of the World: *Punxsutawney, Pennsylvania*

671 Lobster Capital of the World: *Rockland, Maine*

672 Curtain Rod Capital of the World: *Sturgis, Michigan*

673 Sweet Onion Capital of the World: *Vidalia, Georgia*

674 Corncob Pipe Capital of the World: *Washington, Missouri*

675 Broccoli Capital of the World: *Greenfield, California*

676 Toilet Paper Capital of the World: *Green Bay, Wisconsin*

677

The welcoming glow of vintage neon
signs on Mom and Pop motels

ROADSIDE AMERICA

The American road is graced
with countless places to stop and eat,
sleep, shop, fill up, photograph, and write home about.

678
Affordable motels with
air conditioning, plenty of hot water,
cable tv, and an ice machine
right down the hall

679
Free coffee and donuts in the lobby

680
A Gideon Bible in the drawer of
a bedside table in your hotel room

*(and the rumor that there is a $100 bill
tucked inside one of them)*

681
Pet-friendly hotels
and motels

682
The glamour and impeccable
service at the Plaza, the
Waldorf-Astoria and the
Four Seasons hotels in
New York City

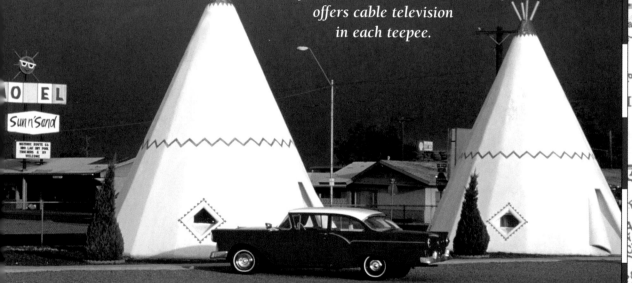

689
Wigwam Motels

The first of the Wigwam Village motels was built by Frank Redford in Kentucky in 1935. His dream was to open a string of motels across the country. Of the seven original villages, only three remain. The one shown here, in Holbrook, Arizona, was refurbished around 1988 and offers cable television in each teepee.

1949 BUSHKILL FALLS PA.

690
Shopping for souvenirs
and gifts to take home to
friends and family,
neighbors,
co-workers
and dog sitters

691
Sending a postcard to a
friend from an exotic location
like Hell, Michigan or
Truth or Consequences,
New Mexico

DEPUTY U.S. MARSHAL

BLACK HILLS, SO. DAK.
MT. RUSHMORE
NEEDLES
MT. RUSHMORE
18 MINIATURE POSTCARDS
FROM ORIGINAL PHOTOGRAPHS

Welcome
DUTCH HAUS
GIFTS
COFFEE SNACKS

692
Toothpick holders, salt and
pepper shakers, plates,
mugs, hats, T-shirts, and
other doodahs to cherish
for a lifetime

693
Stopping for gas and getting
directions from the locals

694
Grabbing a hot cup of coffee and
an evil doughnut

695
Paying at the pump

The Teapot Dome Gas Station, Zilllah, Washington, built in 1922

696 The World's Largest Catsup Bottle, Collinsville, Illinois
Built in 1949, this 170-foot-tall water tower was restored in 1995 and named to the National Register of Historic Places in August 2002.

697 Albert, The World's Largest Bull, Audubon, Iowa
Erected in 1964, Albert, a Hereford bull, weighs 45 tons and stands 30 feet tall.

698 Rawhide, Scottsdale, Arizona
Providing "quality 1880s-style family entertainment" since the 1970s. Gift shops, gun fights, cookouts, and camel rides in the Sonoran Desert.

The Milk Bottle Restaura
Dairy, Taunton, Massach

699 The Corn Palace, Mitchell, South Dakota

Established in 1892, The Corn Palace is a celebration of the bounty of South Dakota. Each year the exterior of the building is covered with murals and designs created from thousands of bushels of corn and other grains grown in South Dakota. It is often called The World's Largest Bird Feeder.

700 Roadside America, Shartlesville, Pennsylvania

The World's Greatest Indoor Miniature Village began as the dream of young Laurence Gieringer. He and his brother began to build miniature houses as children, and Laurence continued to create tiny trolleys, trains, Indian encampments, grist mills, farms and towns for 60 years, until his death in 1963. His family continues his legacy today with a show every 30 minutes that includes the lights of the village coming on at dusk and a recording of Kate Smith singing "God Bless America."

701 Mystery Spots

Located in Santa Cruz, California, Gold Hill, Oregon, St. Ignace, Michigan, and elsewhere, Mystery Spots seem to defy the laws of gravity and physics.

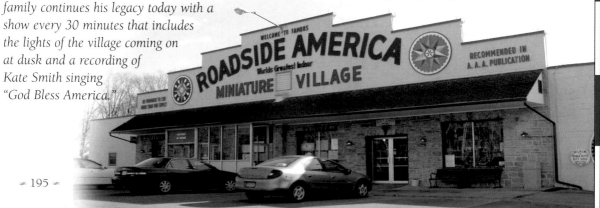

702 The Shoe House

Built in Hellam, Pennsylvania in 1948 by shoe magnate Mahlon "Shoe Wizard" Haines for the purpose of promoting his chain of stores, this wood framed stucco shoe measures 48 feet in length and has three bedrooms, two baths, a kitchen and living room.

703
The World Famous Tree House

Enter this 4,000-year-old redwood and find yourself in a room over 40-feet tall! A fire three centuries ago burned the interior of the tree, but it's still living. This Piercy, California attraction is part of the Avenue of Giants in Northern California.

WORLD FAMOUS TREE HOUSE "BELIEVE IT OR NOT" FRATERNAL MONARCH

VISITORS WELCOME ENTRANCE

101 ft. around. 250 ft. High. "Tallest one-room house in the World".

The American Musical Landscape

Hundreds of American cities, states and regions have inspired songwriters over the years. While California has its share of hits, towns like Gary, Indiana and Galveston, Texas have also been immortalized in song.

Made in America

Throughout the 19th and 20th centuries, American scientists, inventors, and entrepreneurs have created more than their share of innovative products and breakthrough ideas. Earmuffs, telephones, Band-Aids, and air conditioning are a few American innovations we enjoy in our daily lives.

And what about the contribution America has made to the world of music? Jazz, blues, and rock and roll all started here. From Leonard Bernstein to Billy Joel, Louis Armstrong to Elvis Presley, we've been turning out music that brings the world to its feet.

"Made in America" has always been synonymous with innovation and practicality, but we never seem to forget the fun either.

730
The Hula Hoop

Invented in 1957 by Wham-O founders Richard Knerr and Arthur "Spud" Melin. The Hula Hoop, a true American craze, sold 25 million in just two months.

Yankee Ingenuity
American Inventions & Discoveries

What would the world be like without air conditioning, light bulbs, Post-it notes, and the Frisbee? Hot, dark, disorganized and no fun for dogs.

731 Earmuffs

Invented in 1873 by Chester Greenwood of Farmington, Maine. The 15-year-old Greenwood was looking for a way to keep his ears warm while ice skating. Today, Farmington, Maine, is the Earmuff Capital of the world, and December 21 is officially Chester Greenwood Day in Maine.

732 Windshield wipers

Mary Anderson invented the hand-operated windshield wiper in 1903, and patented it in 1905. In 1917, Charlotte Bridgwood invented the first automatic windshield wiper, called "The Storm Windshield Cleaner."

733 Crayola Crayons

Invented by cousins Edwin Binney and C. Harold Smith in Easton, Pennsylvania, they were first sold in 1903, eight colors for a nickel. The name was created by Binney's wife, Alice, who combined the French words for chalk (craie) and oily (oleaginous).

734
The Internet

What is now an international phenomenon of communication and creative potential began in the early 1960s as a response to the Cold War. The United States Air Force commissioned the RAND Corporation to do a study on how the military could maintain control of its weapons following a nuclear attack.

The first network was created in 1969, linking UCLA, UC Santa Barbara and the University of Utah. The first email program was created by Ray Tomlinson in the early 1970s, and the first email message, sent between two computers sitting next to each other, was "QWERTYUIOP," basically the top row of letters on an American keyboard.

735
Bar codes

Invented by Joseph Woodland and Bernard Silver, students at Drexel Institute of Technology in Philadelphia. Patented in 1952, they were first used commercially in 1966. The bar code led the way for the ubiquitous U.P.C., or Uniform Product Code, in use today. The U.P.C. was invented in 1973 by George J. Lauer.

On June 26, 1974, a 10-pack of Wrigley's Juicy Fruit gum made history as the first product ever to be scanned at the checkout counter with a bar code. The gum is on display at the Smithsonian Institution's National Museum of American History.

736
Super Glue

Also known as "Krazy Glue," it was first discovered by Dr. Harry Coover in 1942, and later rediscovered in 1951 by Coover and Dr. Fred Joyner while researching heat-resistant materials for jet canopies.

737
Tupperware

*These nonbreakable, lightweight, airtight, spillproof containers were
invented by Earl Silas Tupper of New Hampshire. It was Brownie Wise
who developed the successful Tupperware Party concept
of direct sales. Party on, girls!*

738 The Heimlich maneuver

Invented by Dr. Henry Heimlich while living in Cincinnati, Ohio, in 1974. This simple anti-choking action has saved countless lives.

739 The shopping cart

The first shopping cart was invented in 1936 by Sylvan Goldman, who owned a chain of Piggly-Wiggly stores in Oklahoma City. His early invention consisted of two wire baskets and wheels attached to a folding chair. In 1946 Orla Watson invented the carts we use today, with the hinged back that allows them to be stored one inside the next.

740 The telephone

The first successful message transmitted by telephone occurred on March 10, 1876 when Alexander Graham Bell spoke to his assistant, saying "Mr. Watson, come here. I want to see you."

741 Toilet paper

Joseph Gayetty of New York is credited with inventing toilet paper in 1857. His concept was later perfected and successfully marketed by Thomas, Edward, and Clarence Scott of Philadelphia when they marketed a small roll of perforated paper. They began the Scott Paper Company by selling their product from a pushcart.

742 Kevlar

Invented by Stephanie Kwolek in 1966. An incredible material five times stronger than steel, Kevlar is used in bulletproof vests, space vehicles, parachutes, and underwater cables.

743 Air conditioning

Invented by Willis Carrier in 1902. While the first applications were for industrial situations, the first installation simply for comfort was in the J.L. Hudson department store of Detroit, Michigan, in 1924. By 1928, Carrier had developed the first air conditioner for the home. Its widespread adoption after World War II changed the way we build houses and made Sunbelt cities like Phoenix, Las Vegas, and Miami inhabitable year-round.

744 Television

Legend has it that the inspiration for television came to Philo Farnsworth at the age of 14 while he was tilling a potato field on his family ranch in Idaho. Moving back and forth with a horse-drawn plow, he had the idea that an electron beam could scan images the same way. On September 7, 1927, he successfully demonstrated his invention and was awarded a patent in 1934.

745 The computer

ENIAC, the first all-purpose electronic digital computer, was built by John William Mauchly and John Presper Eckert Jr. at the University of Pennsylvania in 1945.

Philo Farnsworth, the inventor of television

746 Teflon

Discovered on April 6, 1938, by Dr. Roy Plunkett while working at the DuPont research labs, it came on the market in 1945. Teflon (or tetrafluoroethylene polymer) is made up of some of the largest molecules known, which results in its slippery surface, perfect for frying eggs.

747 Post-it® notes

This everyday staple in American offices and households uses a repositionable adhesive discovered by Dr. Spence Silver at 3M. But the breakthrough came when Art Fry, a new product development researcher, was looking for a bookmark that wouldn't fall out of his hymnal in church. He applied some of Silver's adhesive to a piece of paper and the Post-it note was born! Post-it notes were introduced commercially in 1980.

748 The safety pin

Invented by Walter Hunt in 1849 while fiddling with a piece of wire attempting to make something in order to pay off a $15 bet. The safety pin was patented on April 10, 1849. Perhaps more inventor than businessman, Hunt sold his patent shortly thereafter for $400.

749 Charcoal briquettes

Invented by Henry Ford with assistance from Thomas Edison, they were made from wood scraps and sawdust from Ford's factory.

750 Polaroid photography

Invented by Edwin Herbert Land, it was a revolution in photography. The one-step process of developing and printing the image allowed an instant print. The first Polaroid cameras were sold in November 1948. The 1960s saw the expansion of the marketing of the Polaroid when Land created the Automatic 100 Land Camera, followed by the affordable ($19.95) black and white Polaroid Swinger in 1965. Before digital photography, Polaroid was the only way to see your picture immediately.

control-top pantyhose
safety pins
charcoal briquettes
100-watt light bulbs

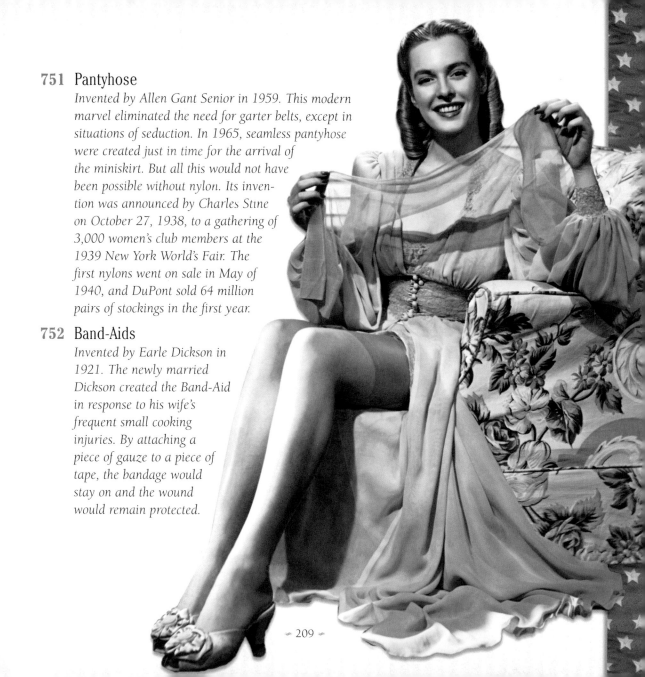

751 Pantyhose

Invented by Allen Gant Senior in 1959. This modern marvel eliminated the need for garter belts, except in situations of seduction. In 1965, seamless pantyhose were created just in time for the arrival of the miniskirt. But all this would not have been possible without nylon. Its invention was announced by Charles Stine on October 27, 1938, to a gathering of 3,000 women's club members at the 1939 New York World's Fair. The first nylons went on sale in May of 1940, and DuPont sold 64 million pairs of stockings in the first year.

752 Band-Aids

Invented by Earle Dickson in 1921. The newly married Dickson created the Band-Aid in response to his wife's frequent small cooking injuries. By attaching a piece of gauze to a piece of tape, the bandage would stay on and the wound would remain protected.

753 Scrabble

First developed by Alfred Butts of New York in the 1930s. He called the game "Lexiko." Its name was changed to "It" and later to "Criss-Cross." The game was refined by James Brunot of Newtown, Connecticut, in 1948. Brunot sold the rights to Selchow & Righter in 1953. The game's popularity soared. Sadly, Alfred Butts, the game's inventor, never earned any money from the most successful board game of the 20th century.

754 The microwave oven

Dr. Percy Spencer invented the microwave while working for the Raytheon Company in 1946. Spencer had been testing a new vacuum tube called a magnetron and noticed that a candy bar in his pocket had melted! He performed an experiment with popcorn and then an egg. The first commercial oven was sold in 1954 and was called the 1161 Radarange. The first countertop microwave oven for the home debuted in 1967, under the name Amana Radarange. It cost under $500 and was to revolutionize the way America cooked. The speed and simplicity of this brilliant machine suited the increasingly fast-paced life of the modern world, and today it is reported that over 90% of American homes have microwave ovens.

755 The mechanical reaper

Invented by Cyrus McCormick in July 1831, this time-and-labor-saving machine changed the way farming was done and created a revolution in agriculture.

756 Q-Tips

Invented in the 1920s by Leo Gerstenzang, a Polish-born American, Q-Tips have been getting into hard-to-reach places for decades. The "Q" in the name stands for "quality."

757 Xerography

Invented in 1938 by Chester Floyd Carlson. It spelled the demise of carbon paper.

758 The light bulb

Created by Thomas Edison in 1879. Although others had previously developed forms of electric lighting, Edison's was the first incandescent light that was safe and practical for home use. It was first publicly demonstrated in December of 1879 at his Menlo Park laboratory.

759 Scotch tape

Invented by Richard Drew in 1930 while working at the 3M Company in St. Paul, Minnesota.

Thomas Alva Edison

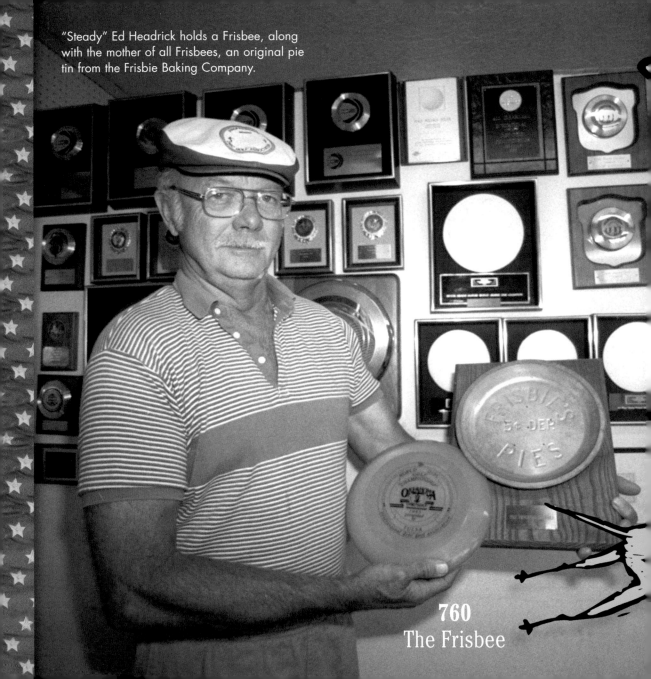

"Steady" Ed Headrick holds a Frisbee, along with the mother of all Frisbees, an original pie tin from the Frisbie Baking Company.

760
The Frisbee

# It's the beautiful flight

The toy of choice for the 1960s youth-and counter-culture was the Frisbee. It represented summer, freedom, and good, clean, affordable anti-gravitational fun. Today's Frisbee has spawned tournaments all over the world and made hundreds of thousands of dogs extremely happy. Its wondrous aerodynamics still make our spirits soar.

The first Frisbee-like toy was invented by Walter "Fred" Morrison and Warren Franscioni in 1948. Marketed as the "Flyin' Saucer," and later the "Pluto Platter," it was inspired by the metal pie tins used by the Frisbie Baking Company of Bridgeport, Connecticut. They were a popular amusement among local college students who would fling them and watch them fly (after they had eaten the pie). Morrison sold the rights to his design to Wham-O founders and marketing geniuses Rich Knerr and Arthur "Spud" Melin in the mid-1950s.

Wham-O began production on January 13, 1957, with the "Pluto Platter" and later renamed their product after the flying pie tins.

Inventor "Steady" Ed Headrick was responsible for the modern aerodynamic design of the professional model that went on sale in 1964. Headrick, an admitted "Frisbyterian," once said, "I felt the Frisbee had some kind of a spirit involved. It's not just like playing catch with a ball. It's the beautiful flight." When he passed away in 2002, he left a request that his ashes be molded into a limited number of flying discs, which would be used to raise money for a future Frisbee and Disc Golf museum.

Whither goest thou, America, in thy shiny car in the night?

Jack Kerouac, On the Road

761
Taking the first drive in a
brand new car

762

The Ford Thunderbird

An icon of American automotive style. Introduced in 1955 as competition for the Chevrolet Corvette, the first T-bird was a two-seater described as a "personal luxury car." Today this sporty car is very popular with collectors.

CLASSIC AMERICAN CARS

America has loved its cars ever since the first Model T Ford rolled off the assembly line. We choose our cars not only for practical applications, but also for the fact that they represent freedom, rugged individualism, and reflect our personal style.

763
Model T Ford
The first mass-produced, affordable automobile. More than any other vehicle, it took America from the horse and buggy era into the modern world of motorized transportation.

764
1949 Mercury
Prized by enthusiasts as a car that lent itself to hot rod modifications.

765
Jeep Wagoneer
One of the earliest four-wheel drive vehicles with a station wagon body, it could be considered the father of today's SUV.

766
1961 Lincoln Continental convertible
This car's styling was considered outstanding at the time.

767 1965 Mustang

A tight four-passenger, high-performance car that put fun back into driving. Now highly collectible, it heralded the beginning of the pony car craze and led the way for the Camaro, Firebird and Barracuda.

768 1957 Plymouth Fury

The ultra-modern styling of Virgil Exner's Chrysler design team influenced other car designers, causing a rush to big tail fins.

769 1957 Chevy

The most loved and sought-after of the '50s classics. It epitomizes the "Fabulous Fifties." (The 1955 Chevy is also a highly popular model.)

770 1960 Corvair

This car is unusual because, like the VW Beetle, it had an air-cooled rear engine with rear-wheel drive. Unfortunately, by the time Chevrolet got the bugs worked out, the car had a poor reliability reputation, and Ralph Nader finished it off with his book, Unsafe at Any Speed.

771 Muscle cars

The 1968 Dodge Charger and the 1969 Pontiac GTO.

772 Dodge minivan, circa 1984

This van started the minivan craze of the '80s, which continues to this day.

773 Dodge Viper

Introduced in the mid 1990s, the Viper is a sports car with a huge V-10 engine.

774
Chevrolet Corvette

*A distinctively American sports car.
Both the two-toned 1957 convertible
and the 1963 split-window Corvette
Stingray are icons of the
American automobile.*

219

775

Finding the perfect car that
reflects our inner self

776 1947 Studebaker

The first car after WWII to display fresh, new styling. It was a giant leap ahead and influenced car design for years to come.

777 1956 Buick Roadmaster

A huge car with lots of chrome and a two-tone paint job. A good example of the styling of the mid 1950s.

778 1965 Oldsmobile Toronado

This stylish car reintroduced front-wheel drive to the American market. Soon every American manufacturer was building front-wheel drive cars.

779 1936 Cord

One of the first high-performance front-wheel drive cars, it is considered by many to be one of the most beautiful cars ever designed.

780 1932-33 Duesenberg

The ultimate large, fast luxury car of its day. These cars were outstanding statements of elegance and good looks. The supercharged model SJ could do up to 130 mph.

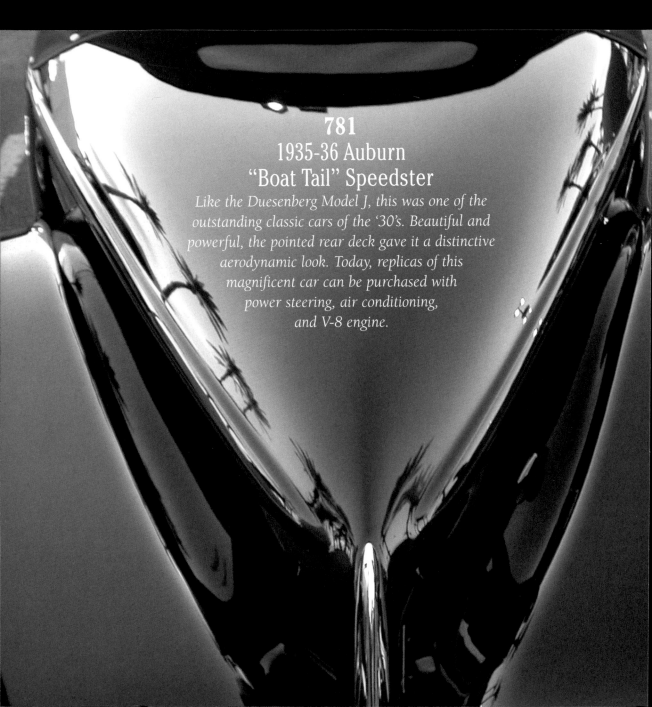

781
1935-36 Auburn
"Boat Tail" Speedster

*Like the Duesenberg Model J, this was one of the
outstanding classic cars of the '30's. Beautiful and
powerful, the pointed rear deck gave it a distinctive
aerodynamic look. Today, replicas of this
magnificent car can be purchased with
power steering, air conditioning,
and V-8 engine.*

782 1914 Stutz Bearcat
One of the first American sports cars. Most popular of its breed, it was successful in the early days of racing.

783 Woodies
The oversized station wagons with wood paneled sides, celebrated in the song "Surf City" by the Beach Boys.

784 1959 Cadillac
The ultimate statement of the outlandish tail fin era and "bigger is better" philosophy. Elvis had a pink Caddy convertible.

785 1968 Pontiac GTO
A classic from the era of muscle cars, it had both looks and "go."

786 The pickup truck
Originally marketed for farmers, ranchers, and small businesses, they are now purchased by every segment of the American population.

787 1937 "Y" Job
A one-of-a-kind dream car built by General Motors as the world's first concept vehicle. It had many new features that appeared years later on production cars, such as concealed running boards, concealed headlamps, and a convertible power top that stored out of sight.

788 1951 Le Sabre
A significant concept vehicle built by GM that previewed a multitude of ideas that would later go into production, such as the wraparound windshield and the first look at the era of tailfins. At $500,000 (1950s dollars), it was one of the most expensive vehicles ever built.

All Aboard!
The American Railroad

The railroad connected America from coast to coast, unifying the nation, bringing a sense of romance to small towns, and making the cross-country journey a great adventure.

789 The Transcontinental Railroad

On May 10, 1869, there was a great celebration at Promontory Point, Utah, as the Central Pacific and Union Pacific engines touched cowcatchers, signaling the completion of the transcontinental railroad. Before the connection of the railroads, a coast-to-coast journey took four to six months. After the two railroads connected, it took six days. In a larger sense, the railroad unified the country in economic, cultural, and political ways.

790 The Super Chief

Beginning in 1936, the Santa Fe Railroad operated the Super Chief from Chicago to Los Angeles. It was renowned for its fine cuisine and was a favorite of Hollywood stars.

791 The California Zephyr

The elegant California Zephyr began Chicago to San Francisco service in 1949. The trip took approximately 2 ½ days and passed through some of America's most spectacular landscapes. Known as "The Silver Lady," it introduced the Vista Dome car, featuring a second story with glass roof panels and providing passengers a better view of mountain scenery.

792 The Broadway Limited

When the Broadway Limited entered service in 1902, it was considered rapid transit, making the run from New York to Chicago in just over 20 hours. In addition to the usual dining car and observation car, it offered a mid-train lounge and six types of private rooms.

These railroads—could but the whistle be made musical,
and the rumble and the jar got rid of—are positively the greatest
blessing that the ages have wrought out for us. They give us wings;
they annihilate the toil and dust of pilgrimage; they
spiritualize travel! Transition being so facile,
what can be any man's inducement
to tarry in one spot?

Nathaniel Hawthorne
The House of the Seven Gables

227

The CENTURY is more than a train—more than a thing of steel and steam and electricity—more than an achievement of American engineering genius. Through twenty-four years of continuous service, the 20TH CENTURY LIMITED has come to represent the spirit of American transportation.

from a promotional postcard, 1925

793
The 20th Century Limited

The 20th Century Limited started New York-to-Chicago service in 1902. It was the New York Central's most luxurious train, featuring Pullman cars with well-appointed bedrooms. A 1914 advertisement claims it offered service equal to the best hotels, with "station telephone connection, stock reports, barber, valet, maid, and stenographer." To welcome passengers, the railroad rolled out a red carpet, giving rise to the phrase the "red carpet treatment."

Words & Music

Great American Songwriters

American songwriters have kept our spirits alive for hundreds of year. Each artist has a unique style and each song is a national treasure to be shared.

794 Stephen Foster

Often called America's First Composer, he was probably the first to make songwriting profitable in the 1800s. We can thank him for "Oh! Susanna," and "Camptown Races."

795 Leonard Bernstein

A songwriter of enormous distinction, he is admired as a composer of classical music, a writer for Broadway, and an innovative music educator for his influential television broadcasts. Bernstein wrote the music for West Side Story, Wonderful Town, *and other musicals.*

796 Sammy Cahn

Born in 1913, Cahn was nominated for more than 30 Oscars and had his songs recorded by almost every major singer of his time. "High Hopes" and "It's Magic" were pure Cahn!

797 George M. Cohan

America's definitive song and dance man was born in 1878, and was a charter member of ASCAP (American Society of Composers, Authors, and Publishers).

Among his patriotic songs is "You're A Grand Old Flag."

798 Duke Ellington

Born into a middle-class black family in 1899, Duke's influence on classical music, popular music, and jazz cannot be over-stated. "It Don't Mean A Thing If It Ain't Got That Swing" and "Solitude" are just two of his gems.

799 Woody Guthrie

An Okie born in 1912, Woodrow Wilson Guthrie had a series of personal tragedies which haunted his life and gave rise to a rambling outlook on life—and music. His "This Land Is Your Land" is an anthem in American music.

800 Billy Joel

This baby boomer, born in 1949, cites everyone from Beethoven to Chopin, from Gershwin to Otis Redding among his influences. One of the most popular artists of our time, Joel is the original "Piano Man," and shared with us his "New York State of Mind."

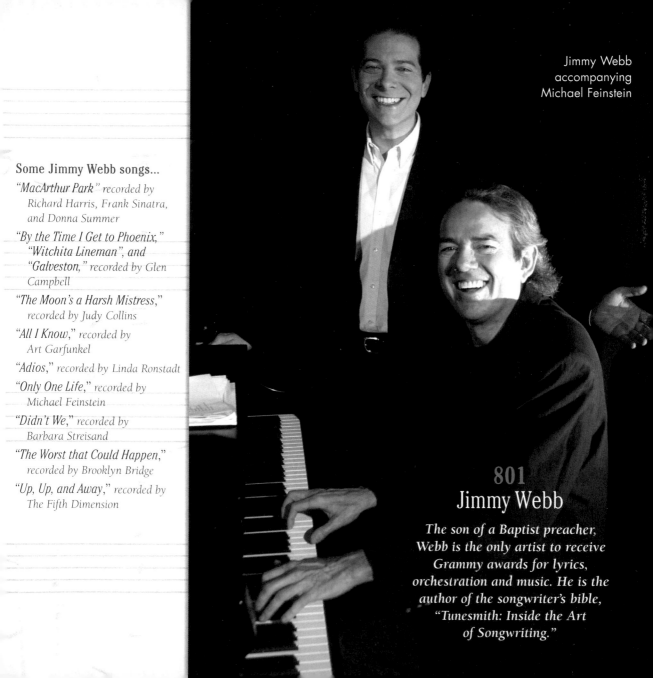

Jimmy Webb
accompanying
Michael Feinstein

Some Jimmy Webb songs...

"MacArthur Park" recorded by
    Richard Harris, Frank Sinatra,
    and Donna Summer

"By the Time I Get to Phoenix,"
    "Witchita Lineman", and
    "Galveston," recorded by Glen
    Campbell

"The Moon's a Harsh Mistress,"
    recorded by Judy Collins

"All I Know," recorded by
    Art Garfunkel

"Adios," recorded by Linda Ronstadt

"Only One Life," recorded by
    Michael Feinstein

"Didn't We," recorded by
    Barbara Streisand

"The Worst that Could Happen,"
    recorded by Brooklyn Bridge

"Up, Up, and Away," recorded by
    The Fifth Dimension

801
Jimmy Webb

*The son of a Baptist preacher,
Webb is the only artist to receive
Grammy awards for lyrics,
orchestration and music. He is the
author of the songwriter's bible,
"Tunesmith: Inside the Art
of Songwriting."*

Hello, Dolly! Wonderful World St. Louis Blues Mood Indigo Ain't Misbehavin' I Got the World on a String Struttin' with Some Barbecue A Kiss to Build a Dream On It Takes Two to Tango That Lucky Old Sun Do You Know What it Means to Miss New Orleans Basin Street Blues

802
Louis Armstrong

Born in New Orleans in 1901, Satchmo brought jazz to a new level with his improvisation and energy.

OF THEE I SING, BABY

AMERICAN MUSIC & MUSICAL GREATS

America's rich musical heritage includes styles as varied as the country itself.
Country western, rock and roll, blues, gospel, and jazz were invented here
and now influence and inspire music everywhere.

803
Jazz

*Jazz is a four-letter word that simply means "cool." Sometimes considered
America's greatest original art form, jazz was born in the late 1890s in New
Orleans, blending ragtime, French quadrilles and blues. The legendary Jelly Roll
Morton claims to have invented jazz at the age of 12. As it evolved, jazz gave us
the Original Dixieland Jazz Band, Louis Armstrong, Duke Ellington, Count Basie,
Billy Holiday, Charlie Parker, Dizzy Gillespie, Miles Davis, John Coltrane,
Ornette Coleman, Thelonious Monk, and many other jazz greats.*

804
Broadway Musicals

From the plains of Oklahoma *to the stirring* Sound of Music. *From the Jets and
Sharks dancing for equal time in* West Side Story, *to the raucous laughter and
swindling of little old ladies in the conniving* The Producers, *American musical
theater emanating from Broadway has entertained audiences for
more than half a century.*

805
Big Band & Swing

*Glenn Miller, Benny Goodman, Tommy Dorsey, and The Andrews Sisters lifted the
spirits of the nation during World War II. Memorable tunes of the period included
"String of Pearls," "Chattanooga Choo-Choo," and "In the Mood."*

... with its steely rhythms, its
rattlety-bang ... I suddenly
heard—and even saw on paper—
the complete construction of the
rhapsody from beginning to end.
I heard it as a sort of musical
kaleidoscope of America—of
our vast melting pot, of our
unduplicated national pep,
of our blues, our
metropolitan madness.

George Gershwin,
describing his train trip and
inspiration for *Rhapsody in Blue*

806
George Gershwin's *Rhapsody in Blue*

American composer George Gershwin began his career at the age of 15 on Tin Pan Alley (28th Street) in New York as a pianist and "song plugger." By 1918 he had a huge hit with his song, "Swanee," followed by a string of successful songs and shows throughout the 1920s. Gershwin was one of the first composers to infuse his music with the rhythms and tonalities of jazz. The Gershwin songbook is filled with American classics such as "I Got Rhythm," "Someone to Watch Over Me," "The Man I Love," "Lady Be Good," and "They Can't Take That Away From Me."

In 1923 Gershwin was invited by conductor Paul Whiteman to write a serious piece of jazz-and-blues-inspired music to be performed the following year in a concert in New York. Gershwin agreed and then forgot about it until January 1924, when his brother Ira saw the concert advertised for February 12, featuring a jazz concerto by George! Now under pressure and with less than three weeks to go, George came up with the basic outline of *Rhapsody in Blue* on the train to Boston and wrote the music in a week. Whiteman's arranger, Ferde Grofé, did the orchestration. The opening glissando of the clarinet is one of the most electrifying moments in American music.

Following the success of *Rhapsody*, Gershwin went on to write his *Concerto in F* (1925) and *An American in Paris* (1928), which included four used taxi horns purchased from Parisian garages to simulate traffic noise, and his opera, *Porgy and Bess* (1935).

Gershwin's music reflected the energy and spirit of America. He once said, "... true music . . . must repeat the thought and aspirations of the people and time. My people are Americans. My time is today."

807
B.B. King

The King of the Blues was born in Indianola, Mississippi, in 1925. With Lucille, his famous guitar, he has recorded hits like "The Thrill is Gone" and "Let the Good Times Roll."

808 The Blues

The blues originated in the South, but found new inspiration and energy when they moved up the river and settled in Chicago. There, a combination of big weather, city life and industrial grit stirred the soul. Some great American blues artists include Robert Johnson (Sweet Home Chicago, Cross Road Blues), John Lee Hooker ("Boom Boom," "Boogie Chillen No. 2," and "One Bourbon, One Scotch, One Beer"); Muddy Waters ("I Feel Like Going Home"); Howlin' Wolf ("Back Door Man"); and Buddy Guy & Junior Wells ("Drinkin' TNT Smokin Dynamite").

809 Gospel music

Gospel music was commonly performed in churches in black communities during the first half of the twentieth century. It was not associated with blues and jazz, despite the similarity of their origins. The great Mahalia Jackson personified gospel music, and sang just before Dr. Martin Luther King Jr. delivered his "I Have a Dream" speech in 1963. James Cleveland, The Dixie Hummingbirds, The Mighty Clouds of Joy, and countless others brought Americans inspiration and comfort over the years.

810 Ragtime

Piano rags, in strictly syncopated two-four time, preceded traditional jazz. Scott Joplin was one of ragtime's founding fathers, and his lively "Maple Leaf Rag" and "The Entertainer" are two great American piano pieces.

811
Boogie Woogie

Even before Prohibition the house-rent party flourished in Chicago's South Side. When rent day drew near often the only way to pay the landlord was to throw a party, which was called "pitchin' boogie." That meant open house for the entire neighborhood. The only entrance fee was fifty cents and a sack of sandwiches, or a jug of gin. One person who never had to bring any half-dollar, nor even his own gin, was Jimmy Yancey. He was always welcome. Jimmy, a born comedian and an old vaudeville trouper, was the life of the party. Around five o'clock in the morning, when almost everyone was knocked out and things were getting pretty dull and awfully quiet, someone over in a corner came to life and yelled out, "Let's have some blues." Then Jimmy obliged with his "Five O'Clock Blues," known as the "Fives" for short. No one called it Boogie Woogie then, but it had all the peculiarites of the piano style known today as Boogie Woogie.

William Russell, *Boogie Woogie*
from *Jazzmen*

812   The honky-tonk songs of Hank Williams: "Your Cheatin' Heart," "Hey, Good Lookin' " and "Why Don't You Love Me Like You Used to Do?"

813   Bob Wills and his Texas Playboys and their western swing sounds on "Right or Wrong" and "New San Antonio Rose"

814   Bill Monroe's bluegrass classic, "Blue Moon of Kentucky"

815   Willie Nelson's "Night Life," "On the Road Again," "Blue Eyes Crying in the Rain," and "Always On My Mind"

816   Johnny Paycheck's rendition of "Take This Job and Shove It"

817   Lester Flatt and Earl Scruggs' spectacular combination of banjo, old-time fiddle and guitar on "Foggy Mountain Breakdown"

818   The Highwaymen performing "Mamas Don't Let Your Babies Grow Up to be Cowboys"

819   Patsy Cline's "Crazy"

820   Tammy Wynette's "Divorce" and "Stand By Your Man"

821   Loretta Lynn's "Coal Miner's Daughter"

822   Waylon Jennings, Porter Waggoner, Garth Brooks, Tim McGraw, Vince Gill, Dwight Yoakam, Merle Haggard, Conway Twitty, Buck Owens, Randy Travis, Charlie Pride, Kenny Rogers, and all the great men of country music

823
The great Johnny Cash
and his recordings of
"Folsom Prison Blues,"
"Ring of Fire"
and "I Walk the Line"

237

824
Patsy Cline,
Maybelle Carter,
Dolly Parton,
Loretta Lynn,
Tammy Wynette,
Reba McEntire,
Emmy Lou Harris,
The Dixie Chicks,
LeAnn Rimes,
Shania Twain
and all the great
women of
country music

"Country music is three chords and the truth."

Harlan Howard

832
The tradition of the singing cowboy

Many of America's great western songs were first introduced in cowboy films of the 1930s and '40s. One of the most successful and prolific of the singing cowboys was Gene Autry. Inspired by the singing of Jimmy Rodgers, Autry billed himself as "Oklahoma's Singing Cowboy," and began a recording career in 1929.

Autry appeared in 93 films including *South of the Border* (1939) and *The Last Round Up* (1947); had a television show that ran for five years in the 1950s; and had a weekly radio show called *Melody Ranch.* His western classics include "Back in the Saddle Again," "Silver Haired Daddy of Mine," and "You Are My Sunshine."

Gene Autry's honest, familiar voice was a holiday tradition in the beloved recordings of "Here Comes Santa Claus" (1947), "Peter Cottontail" (1950), and "Rudolph the Red-Nosed Reindeer"(1949).

Roy Rogers, the King of the Cowboys, performed and recorded music with his group, the Sons of the Pioneers. "Empty Saddles," "Cool Water," and "Tumbling Tumbleweeds" showcased their cowboy harmonies. Rogers went on to a career in movies, television, and solo recording. His signature song, performed with his wife, Dale Evans, was "Happy Trails," written by Dale Evans.

Gene Autry's Cowboy Creed

A cowboy never takes unfair advantage —
even of an enemy.

A cowboy never betrays a trust.
He never goes back on his word.

A cowboy always tells the truth.

A cowboy is kind and gentle to small
children, old folks, and animals.

A cowboy is free from racial and
religious intolerances.

A cowboy is always helpful when
someone is in trouble.

A cowboy is always a good worker.

A cowboy respects womanhood,
his parents and his nation's laws.

A cowboy is clean about his person in
thought, word, and deed.

A cowboy is a patriot.

833
American Bandstand

From its beginnings in the mid-1950s, American Bandstand and Dick Clark brought America's youth the latest music, dances, and fashions. Originally filmed in Philadelphia at 46th and Market Street, it aired every week day afternoon for six years. The show lasted 33 years.

The Music World Exploded

If it is possible to identify a moment in which rock and roll emerged as a powerful movement, one would have to pick July 9, 1955. *Cherry Pink and Apple Blossom White* slipped from the number one single and was replaced by

Rock Around the Clock

by Bill Haley and the Comets, originally a country and western group who identified "Rock Around the Clock" on the record label as a "Fox Trot." The identification as a fox trot notwithstanding, the music world exploded. Rock and roll had arrived.

Tom Dalzell
*Flappers 2 Rappers,
American Youth Slang*

243

834
All-time great songs from the golden era of rock and roll

1954-1955

Rock Around The Clock, *Bill Haley and His Comets*

Shake, Rattle and Roll, *Joe Turner*

Maybellene, *Chuck Berry*

Tutti-Frutti, *Little Richard*

Ain't That A Shame, *Fats Domino*

1956

Blue Suede Shoes, *Carl Perkins*

Roll Over Beethoven, *Chuck Berry*

Be-Bop-A-Lula, *Gene Vincent*

Why Do Fools Fall In Love, *Frankie Lymon & the Teenagers*

Hound Dog, *Elvis Presley*

1957

Whole Lotta Shakin' Goin' On, *Jerry Lee Lewis*

All Shook Up, *Elvis Presley*

Jailhouse Rock, *Elvis Presley*

At the Hop, *Danny and the Juniors*

Little Bitty Pretty One, *Thurston Harris*

C.C. Rider, *Chuck Willis*

Peggy Sue, *Buddy Holly*

That'll Be The Day, *Buddy Holly*

Great Balls of Fire, *Jerry Lee Lewis*

1958

Johnny B. Goode, *Chuck Berry*

Summertime Blues, *Eddie Cochran*

Good Golly, Miss Molly, *Little Richard*

Get A Job, *The Silhouettes*

Rockin' Robin, *Bobby Day*

Chantilly Lace, *Big Bopper*

1959

Donna, *Ritchie Valens*

Dream Lover, *Bobby Darin*

16 Candles, *The Crest*

A Big Hunk O' Love, *Elvis Presley*

1960

Only The Lonely, *Roy Orbison*

The Twist, *Chubby Checker*

Save the Last Dance for Me, *The Drifters*

1961

Runaway, *Del Shannon*

Blue Moon, *The Marcels*

Runaround Sue, *Dion*

Peppermint Twist, *Joey Dee and The Starliters*

1962

Duke of Earl, *Gene Chandler*

The Loco-Motion, *Little Eva*

Up on the Roof, *The Drifters*

Surfin' Safari, *The Beach Boys*

Sherry, *The Four Seasons*

1963

Surf City, *Jan and Dean*

Easier Said Than Done, *The Essex*

One Fine Day, *The Chiffons*

He's So Fine, *The Chiffons*

Wipe Out, *The Surfaris*

It's My Party, *Leslie Gore*

Louie, Louie, *The Kingsmen*

1964

Pretty Woman, *Roy Orbison*

Dancing in the Street, *Martha and the Vandellas*

Leader of the Pack, *The Shangri-Las*

She's Not There, *The Zombies*

Chapel of Love, *The Dixie Cups*

Little Old Lady from Pasadena, *Jan and Dean*

1965

The Name Game, *Shirley Ellis*

Help Me, Rhonda, *The Beach Boys*

You've Lost That Lovin' Feelin',
   The Righteous Brothers

Woolly Bully,
   Sam the Sham and the Pharoahs

I Got You Babe, *Sonny & Cher*

1966

Wild Thing, *The Troggs*

When a Man Loves a Woman,
   Percy Sledge

Monday, Monday,
   The Mamas & the Papas

Good Vibrations, *The Beach Boys*

Devil with a Blue Dress On,
   Mitch Ryder & the Detroit Wheels

1967

Soul Man, *Sam & Dave*

Respect, *Aretha Franklin*

Happy Together, *The Turtles*

The Letter, *The Box Tops*

835
Elvis Presley, The King

The American Dream

From poor immigrants turned millionaires to Hollywood actors who become presidents and governors, America's story is one of ordinary people achieving extraordinary dreams.

But dreams need not be so lofty. Owning your own home, putting the kids through college, starting a business, writing a novel, or finally retiring to a quiet, lakeside cottage are all familiar examples of the American dream. All it takes is a vision, some hard work, a little bit of luck, and the freedom to try.

COMING HOME

Millions of Americans share the dream of owning their own home. But a house is not a home. Home is so much more. It is a family gathering place, a caring community, good neighbors, local pride, familiar surroundings, and a place to express your personal style.

836 A "Home, Sweet Home" sign embroidered by your grandmother

837 A cozy log cabin filled with rustic furniture made of pine logs

838 A classic ranch house with a big dog sleeping on the porch

839 A contemporary dream home on the California coast

840 A traditional New England Cape Cod house with window boxes filled with flowers

841 A starter home with a mortgage you can afford

842 A big, bright apartment with lots of closets and your own parking space

843
A great neighborhood where we
make lifelong friends

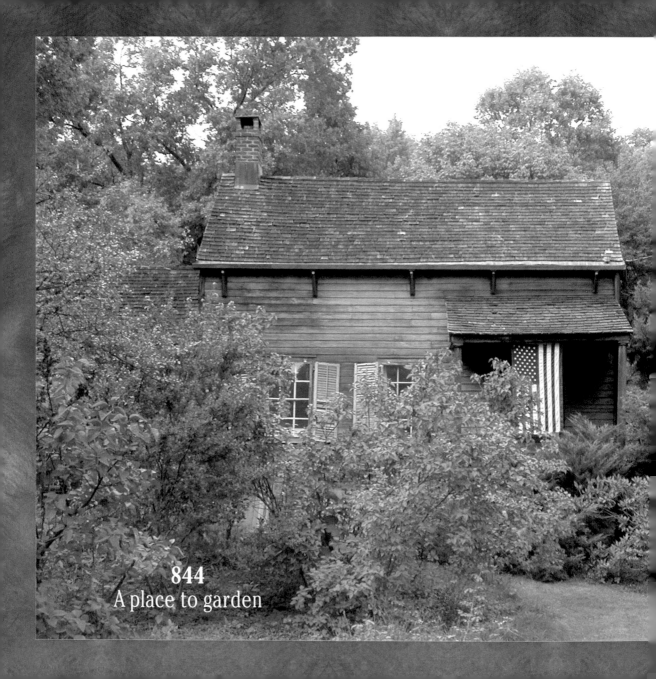

844
A place to garden

THE DREAM OF CREATING A BUSINESS

Calvin Coolidge once said, "The chief business of the American people is business."
For many Americans, the dream of starting their own business means independence, the possibility
of financial success and the chance to show the world what they can do. And many American companies,
like the ones listed here, have revolutionized the way the world communicates,
works, shops, eats, travels, and lives.

EBAY	DUPONT	YAHOO
AMAZON	CITIBANK	GOOGLE
MCDONALD'S	LEVI STRAUSS & CO.	GENERAL MOTORS
STARBUCKS	JOHN DEERE	FORD
APPLE COMPUTER	MICROSOFT	CHRYSLER
WALT DISNEY	INTEL	GILETTE
COCA-COLA	MOTOROLA	H.J. HEINZ
WAL-MART	SUN MICROSYSTEMS	HOME DEPOT
AMERICAN AIRLINES	PROCTER & GAMBLE	FEDEX
SOUTHWEST AIRLINES	UNITED TECHNOLOGIES	XEROX
JET BLUE	IBM	3M
AT&T	DELL	NIKE
SEARS, ROEBUCK AND CO.	PEPSI-COLA	BOEING
ANHEUSER-BUSCH	JOHNSON & JOHNSON	EASTMAN KODAK
AMERICAN EXPRESS	PFIZER	
CATERPILLAR	MERCK	
BRISTOL-MYERS SQUIBB	ELI LILLY	
BANK OF AMERICA	GENERAL ELECTRIC	
THE GAP	COSTCO	

The dream of opening
a retail business

Andrew Carnegie
began his life in poverty.
Emigrating from Scotland with
his family in 1848, Carnegie went on to
build an empire of steel, becoming the richest
man in the world when he sold his company to J.P.
Morgan in 1901 for $480,000,000. Carnegie often
said that "the man who dies rich dies disgraced," and
went on to give away his fortune, establishing institutions
that help people help themselves. At the end of his life,
he had given away $350,000,000.

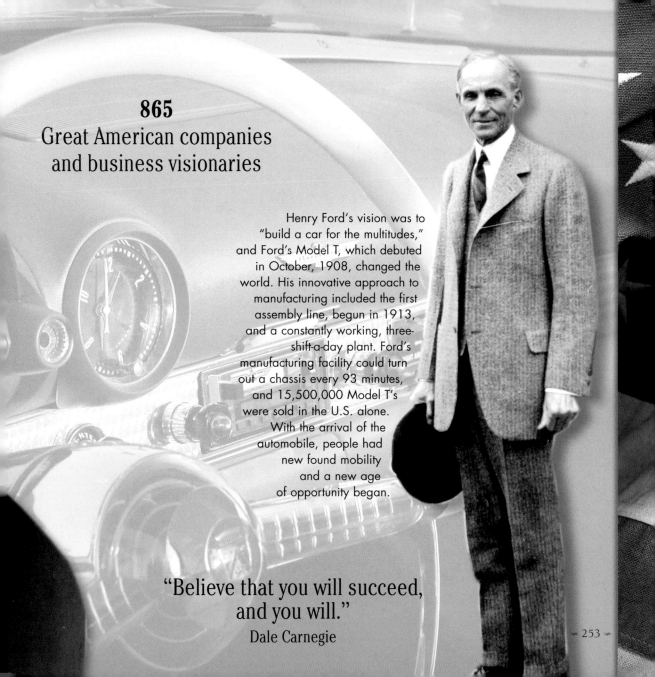

865
Great American companies and business visionaries

Henry Ford's vision was to "build a car for the multitudes," and Ford's Model T, which debuted in October, 1908, changed the world. His innovative approach to manufacturing included the first assembly line, begun in 1913, and a constantly working, three-shift-a-day plant. Ford's manufacturing facility could turn out a chassis every 93 minutes, and 15,500,000 Model T's were sold in the U.S. alone. With the arrival of the automobile, people had new found mobility and a new age of opportunity began.

"Believe that you will succeed, and you will."
Dale Carnegie

866
The nightly wonder of
a desert sunset

The American West
A Dream of the Frontier

The rugged beauty of the western landscape and the romance of the lone cowboy riding the range inspire thoughts of freedom and individuality. The frontier has always been a place where dreams reside.

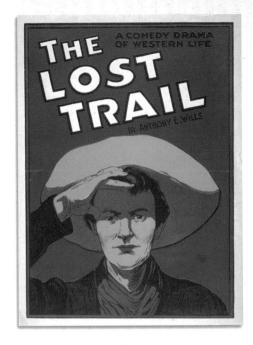

887
The ancient dwellings of
Mesa Verde

Home on the Range

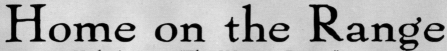

Brewster Higley's poem, "The Western Poem,"
was published in a Kansas newspaper
in December 1893.

Oh, give me a home
Where the buffalo roam
Where the deer and
   the antelope play,
Where seldom is heard
A discouraging word,
And the sky is not cloudy all day.

Home, home on the range
Where the deer and the
   antelope play,
Where seldom is heard a
   discouraging word
And the sky is not cloudy all day.

888
Great Western Songs

Red River Valley

San Antonio Rose

Tumbling Tumbleweeds

Ragtime Cowboy Joe

Buffalo Gals

I'm an Old Cowhand from
the Rio Grande

Don't Fence Me In

Happy Trails

INTO THE WILD BLUE YONDER

America's thirst for freedom and exploration has taken us
to new frontiers in the skies and beyond.

889
Amelia Earhart

*Earhart was one of the most famous women of her time. Her
many record-breaking flights included becoming the first
woman to fly solo across the Atlantic in 1932 and the Pacific in
1935. Her 1937 round-the-world flight attempt ended with her
disappearance somewhere in the South Pacific.*

890
Boeing B-17 Flying Fortress

*The B-17 is perhaps the best known of the heavy bombers
flown by the U.S. Air Force on missions over occupied Europe
during World War II. When the B-17 was first shown to the
public, a reporter looked at all the defensive guns bristling from
the plane and said, "It looks like a flying fortress." Boeing liked
the name and adopted it for the B-17.*

891
Charles Lindbergh and
The Spirit of St. Louis

*Lindbergh entered the history books on
May 21, 1927, when he arrived in Paris,
completing the first solo nonstop
transatlantic flight in history. Lindbergh
and his plane, The Spirit of St. Louis,
became an international sensation.
Today, the Spirit of St. Louis is housed
at the National Air and Space
Museum in Washington, DC.*

892 **The Wright Brothers**

The Wright brothers' Flyer with Orville at the controls made aviation history on December 17, 1903. It successfully made the first controlled flight at 10:35am at Kitty Hawk, North Carolina, flying 120 feet in 12 seconds. Made of wood, fabric and wire, it resides today in the National Air and Space Museum in Washington, DC.

Air Force One flying over Mt. Rushmore

262

893 Air Force One: the presidential plane

There are actually two Boeing 747-200B series aircraft designated as Air Force One. These more-than comfortable jets can carry over 70 passengers halfway around the world without refueling.

894 Boeing 707

Boeing was the first American company to develop a jet-powered commercial airliner. The resulting 707, since it was much faster and quieter, rendered piston-powered airliners obsolete.

895 Boeing 747

This was the first jumbo jet. It has a gross weight of 805,000 pounds and can carry up to 500 passengers. The 747 can be recognized by the hump on the front of the fuselage that contains the flight deck and a first-class lounge.

896 Douglas DC-3

Soon after deliveries began in 1936, the DC-3 became the most widely used airliner because of its advanced design. The military quickly recognized the airplane's potential as a troop and cargo carrier. The government purchased about 10,000 DC-3s during World War II, calling them the C-47. After the war ended, airlines bought the airplanes as soon as they were declared surplus by the military. Despite the fact that the last DC-3 was built in 1948, about 1,000 are still flying today.

897 Ford Tri-Motor

In the 1920s flying on an airliner was considered a high-risk adventure. So, Henry Ford set out to produce a sturdy-looking dependable airplane that would attract more passengers. The Tri-motor was designed with three engines because engines were not yet very dependable. If one engine failed, the Tri-motor would be able to continue flying on the remaining two. Unlike many airliners of the time, the Tri-motor featured all-metal construction. The corrugated, rather than smooth, metal skin of the airplane provided additional strength. The Depression brought production to an end in 1933.

898 Grumman F-14 Tomcat

This carrier-based aircraft's primary role is as a long-range interceptor protecting the fleet. Its most unusual feature is the variable sweep of the wings. They are swept back only 20 degrees during low-speed flight. As the F-14 increases its speed, the wings automatically sweep back to as much as 68 degrees. This extreme sweep angle allows the current model of the F-14 to achieve the extraordinary speed of nearly 1,800 miles per hour.

899 Boeing B-52 Stratofortress

One of the most remarkable aspects of this long-range bomber is its longevity. The last B-52 was delivered to the USAF in 1962. However, by virtue of continual updating of the aircraft, the USAF will continue to fly the B-52 well into the 21st century.

900 Learjet 23

This was one of the first twin jet executive aircraft. While many of the piston-engine powered executive aircraft were larger, the Learjet's much faster economical cruising speed of 485 miles per hour assured its success.

TOP: B-52 Stratofortress; ABOVE: F-14 Tomcat

901 Lockheed SR-71 Blackbird
*During the Cold War,
which began shortly after
World War II and lasted
until the breakup of the
Soviet Union, the U.S.
and its allies were very
concerned about the capa-
bilities of the Soviets and
other communist nations. The
SR-71, from 1966 through 1989,
served as the ultimate spy plane.
Since it was capable of cruising at
2,300 miles per hour at 85,000 feet, none
were lost to hostile missile attack, despite
numerous attempts.*

902
Bell X-1: Glamorous Glennis

This rocket-propelled research aircraft was the first to break the sound barrier in level flight. Captain Chuck Yeager reached a speed of 1.05 Mach, 670 miles per hour at 42,000 feet on October 14, 1947. Yeager named the aircraft "Glamorous Glennis" in honor of his wife.

903 Lockheed P-38 Lightning

One of the most distinctive looking aircraft flown by American pilots during World War II was the P-38. It was a twin-engine fighter. The pilot's compartment was situated on the wing center section and a fuselage, or boom, extended back from each engine. At the back end of each boom was a vertical tail. These tails were linked together by a horizontal tailplane. The twin tail design of the P-38 inspired tailfins on American automobiles after the war.

904 North American F-86 Sabre

Entering service in 1948, the F-86 was the first American sweptwing jet fighter. This very successful aircraft was used by a number of allied countries and saw extensive service during the Korean War (1950-1953).

905 North American P-51 Mustang

The P-51 is probably the most famous American fighter of World War II. While the 15,000 Mustangs built served many roles, the P-51's unusually long range allowed it to serve as a bomber escort for raids deep into Germany.

906 F-117 Nighthawk

Suspected by aircraft aficionados to be in existence since the early 1980s, the super-secret F-117 Nighthawk stealth precision strike aircraft made its first official debut during Operation Desert Storm in 1991. The revolutionary design is a product of Lockheed's legendary "Skunk Works" development center in Burbank, California.

907 Piper J-3 Cub: In 1937

In 1937 Piper started building this in expensive light airplane for use by private pilots. It rapidly became very popular. During World War II the U.S. military re-named it the L-4 Grasshopper and employed it for aerial reconnaissance and many other duties.

908
The Thunderbirds
of the U.S. Air Force

909
The Blue Angels

The United States Navy's precision flying team.

Jacqueline Cochran stands on the wing of the F-86 while talking to Chuck Yeager and Canadair's chief test pilot, Bill Longhurst.

910 Jacqueline "Jackie" Cochran

Test pilot Jacqueline Cochran was hooked on flying at an early age. In addition to a long list of aeronautical accomplishments, she set three speed records, was the first to fly above 33,000 feet, and became the first female trans-Atlantic bomber pilot during World War II. When Cochran was over 50 years old, she became the first woman to break the sound barrier in an F-86 Sabre Jet and later set a world speed record of 1,329 mph in 1964.

911

The Apollo 11 Mission to the Moon

On July 20, 1969, Neil Armstrong was the first man to set foot on the surface of the moon.

Neil Armstrong photographed lunar module pilot Edwin "Buzz" Aldrin during their 2 ½ hour moonwalk.

The Hubble Space Telescope

Launched on April 25, 1990, the Hubble has been sending back images that witness the birth of stars, and deep field images that take us back in time more than 10 billion years.

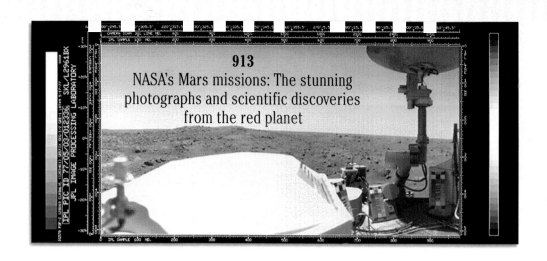

913
NASA's Mars missions: The stunning photographs and scientific discoveries from the red planet

AMERICAN WRITERS & ARTISTS

Countless writers and artists have shared with us their unique visions of America through novels, plays, poems, short stories, painting, sculpture and photography.

920 Washington Irving (1783-1859)

One of the first Americans to be recognized abroad as a man of letters, Irving became a literary idol at home.

His two most famous stories, "The Legend of Sleepy Hollow" and "Rip Van Winkle" (1820), made him the first American to earn his living by writing, and the first to gain world fame.

921 James Fenimore Cooper (1789-1851)

In his Leatherstocking Tales, a series of four novels, Cooper dramatized the clash between the frontier wilderness and encroaching civilization. He was the first important American writer to use subjects and landscapes of his native land to create a vivid myth of frontier life.

922 Nathaniel Hawthorne (1804-1864)

One of the great masters of American fiction, Hawthorne used his novels to explore spiritual and moral conflicts. The Scarlet Letter (1850) is considered the first American psychological novel.

923 William Faulkner (1897-1962)

Awarded the 1949 Nobel Prize in literature, he is ranked among the great American writers of the twentieth century. Faulkner's primary interest was the deep South. In his novels, Faulkner examines the effects of the loss of traditional values and authority on all levels of Southern society.

924 John Steinbeck (1902-1968)

He is best remembered for his strong sociological novel The Grapes of Wrath (1939), which gained him a Pulitzer Prize. It chronicled the plight of Dust Bowl farmers in the 1930s.

925 Eugene O'Neill (1888-1953)

O'Neill is widely acknowledged as America's greatest playwright. In 1931 his famous trilogy, Mourning Becomes Electra, was produced, and in 1936 he received the Nobel Prize in literature.

926 Herman Melville (1819-1891)

Acknowledged as one of the great American writers and a major figure in world literature, Melville's masterpiece, Moby Dick (1851), is an exciting story of whaling and the sea, as well as a philosophical inquiry into the nature of good and evil.

927 Mark Twain (Samuel Langhorne Clemens, 1835-1910) **The Adventures of Huckleberry Finn (1884)** *is a masterpiece of humor, characterization, and realism and has been called the first modern American novel. A writer and humorist who dealt with politics, racism, and national identity, Twain often used Missouri and the Mississippi River— where he spent his boyhood years—as settings.*

928

The Adventures of
Huckleberry Finn

Sometimes we'd have that whole river to ourselves

Sometimes we'd have that whole river to ourselves, for the longest time. Yonder was the banks and the islands, across the water; and maybe a spark— which was a candle in a cabin window—and sometimes on the water you could see a spark or two—on a raft or a scow, you know; and maybe you could hear a fiddle or a song coming over from one of them crafts. It's lovely to live on a raft . . . Once or twice of a night we could see a steamboat slipping along in the dark, and now and then she would belch a whole world of sparks up out of her chimbleys, and they would rain down in the river and look awful pretty; then she would turn a corner and her lights would wink out and her pow-wow shut off and leave the river still again; and by and by her waves would get to us, a long time after she was gone, and joggle the raft a bit, and after that you wouldn't hear nothing for you couldn't tell how long except maybe frogs or something.

After midnight the people on shore went to bed, and then for two or three hours the shores was black— no more sparks in the cabin windows. These sparks was our clock—the first one that showed, again, meant morning was coming, so we hunted a place to hide and tie up, right away.

Mark Twain,
The Adventures of Huckleberry Finn

Hemingway at his home
in Sun Valley, Idaho, 1939,
working on his novel,
For Whom the Bell Tolls.

929 Ernest Hemingway (1899-1961)
Acknowledged as one of the great American writers of the twentieth century, Hemingway wrote about people who handled danger and challenges with stoic courage. Hemingway's novel The Sun Also Rises *(1926)—the definitive statement of the effect of World War I and its aftermath on American and European intellectuals—caused him to be called the spokesman of the "lost generation."* A Farewell to Arms *(1929) was the most striking of the many anti-war novels of the decade.*

930 Tennessee Williams (1911-1983)
One of America's foremost playwrights, he is considered a symbolic poet of the theater. His first success was The Glass Menagerie *(1945), and he won a Pulitzer Prize for* A Streetcar Named Desire *(1947).*

931 Arthur Miller (1915-)
His masterpiece, Death of a Salesman *(1949), earned him a Pulitzer Prize. Miller's plays are concerned with morality and the pressures exerted on people by family and society.*

932 F. Scott Fitzgerald *(1896-1940)*

A novelist and short story writer, Fitzgerald earned a place as one of the best American writers of last century. His most famous novel, The Great Gatsby (1925) presents a withering portrait of the so-called American Dream which measures success and love in terms of money. Tender Is the Night (1934), an examination of American mores and personal values as well as emotional loss, is lauded for its lyrical, imaginative writing. Fitzgerald was widely considered to be the literary spokesman of the "Jazz Age"—the decade of the 1920s.

Human life itself may be almost pure chaos, but the work of the artist is to take these handfuls of confusion and disparate things, things that seem to be irreconcilable, and put them together in a frame to give them some kind of shape and meaning.

Katherine Anne Porter

933 Walt Whitman (1819-1892)
His Leaves of Grass (1855) is considered one of the most influential volumes of poems in the history of American literature. Whitman celebrated the freedom and dignity of the individual and sang the praises of democracy and the brotherhood of man.

934 Emily Dickinson (1830-1886)
Not discovered until after her death, Dickinson's poems reflect her doubts about orthodox religion and her toward transcendentalism and her longing for spiritual comfort from it.

935 Jack Kerouac (1922-1969)
A prominent figure of the Beat Generation, his novel On the Road (1957) is considered a testament of the Beat movement.

936 Edward Hopper (1882-1967)
A pioneer of American realism and a master of light, Hopper's work portrays a sense of isolation and loneliness in the modern world. His painting Nighthawks (1942) was inspired by a diner in Greenwich Village in New York, where he lived for over 50 years.

937 Norman Rockwell (1894-1978)
Rockwell was a painter and illustrator who created art for the covers of the Saturday Evening Post and other magazines. In 1942, inspired by a speech given by FDR, Rockwell created a series of paintings called the Four Freedoms. The paintings represented Freedom of Speech, Freedom of Worship, Freedom from Want, and Freedom from Fear.

938 Ansel Adams (1902-1984)
His eloquent photographs capture the light and natural forms of western landscapes.

939 Georgia O'Keefe (1887-1986)
O'Keefe's extraordinary paintings of New York, the Southwest, and langer-than-life flowers encourage us to see the world of forms in a truly different way. In 1976 she received the Medal of Freedom from President Gerald Ford.

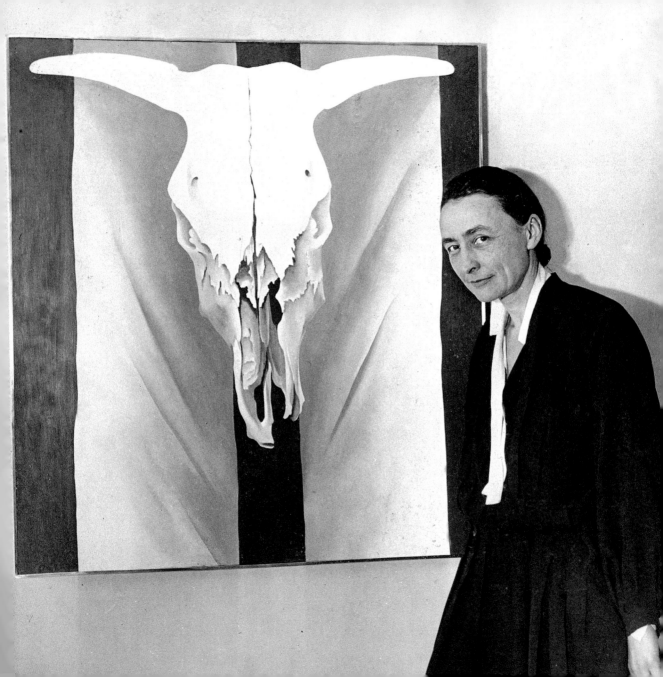

940
Visual artists and designers
who changed the way we
see the world

Milton Avery

Jean-Michel Basquiat

Thomas Hart Benton

Alexander Calder

George Catlin

Currier and Ives

Thomas Eakins

Milton Glaser

Winslow Homer

Jasper Johns

Roy Lichtenstein

Annie Liebowitz

Peter Max

Thomas Moran

Louise Nevelson

Jackson Pollock

Robert Rauschenberg

Frederic Remington

Larry Rivers

Mark Rothko

John Singer Sargent

Charles Schultz

David Smith

Edward Steichen

Alfred Stieglitz

Frank Stella

Louis Sullivan

Andy Warhol

Edward Weston

James Whistler

Margaret Bourke White

Grant Wood

Frank Lloyd Wright

Andrew Wyeth

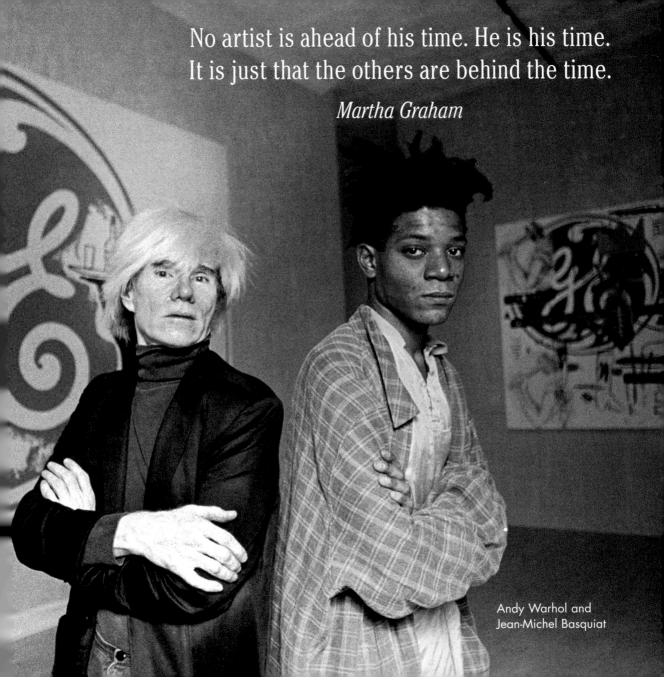

No artist is ahead of his time. He is his time.
It is just that the others are behind the time.

Martha Graham

Andy Warhol and
Jean-Michel Basquiat

941
Edward Curtis
(1868-1952)

Known as "Shadow Catcher" by
many of the Native Americans he
photographed, Edward Curtis
recorded the faces and the ways of
life of over eighty tribal groups.
His collection comprises over
40,000 images of great beauty
and rare information.

Preserving Our Wilderness

From the old growth forests of the Northwest to the Florida Everglades, America is blessed with large and diverse wilderness areas. The primeval beauty of these lands is the legacy of many past visionaries. Today, we all share the responsibility to preserve, improve, and pass on their gift to future generations.

942
The environmental groups, large and small, who work to preserve and protect our land and its animals

943
Henry David Thoreau

Author of Walden *(1854), an account of his two years spent at Walden Pond. Part scientist, part philosopher, he saw that we derive strength from our connection with the natural world. During a time of expansion and exploitation of the land, Thoreau urged the government to set aside areas that would be kept wild and preserved for future generations.*

944
Rachel Carson

Scientist and author of Silent Spring *(1962). Her startling account of the hazards of pesticide use (DDT) started the environmental movement in America.*

I have run
live, I'll he₂
birds an
interpret
the l₂
storm, an
I'll acquain
glaciers ₂
and get as
th

945
John Muir

Nature writer, father of our national parks, and founder of the Sierra Club. On a camping trip in 1903 in Yosemite, Muir persuaded President Theodore Roosevelt to establish the U.S. Forest Service.

As long as I
terfalls and
ds sing. I'll
rocks, learn
ge of flood,
avalanche.
elf with the
d gardens,
he heart of
d as I can.

John Muir

946
The Nature Conservancy
*Since 1951, it has been working to
preserve the plants, animals, and
natural communities that represent
the diversity of life on Earth by
protecting the lands and waters
they need to survive.*

Glacier National Park

947
The Sierra Club

Founded by John Muir and others on May 28, 1892, the Sierra Club has worked to protect our wild places. With 700,000 members, it is America's oldest, largest, and most influential grass-roots environmental organization.

948
John Wesley Powell

Explorer, geologist, anthropologist and conservationist, he navigated the Colorado River through the Grand Canyon in 1869, covering nearly 1,000 miles of wild, uncharted river. After his second expedition, in 1871, he produced a detailed map and several scientific papers.

949
Pete Seeger

Musician Pete Seeger used his talents to champion a cause he believed in. In 1966 he decided to save the Hudson River. The great river had become polluted with raw sewage, oil, and industrial chemicals. Seeger's sloop, the Clearwater, sailed to Washington, DC, in 1970 to plead the case for the Hudson and all waterways. Through songs, speeches and petitions he galvanized support for the Clean Water Act which was passed in 1972 and signed into law by President Richard Nixon.

950
William Henry Jackson

He was the first photographer to record the unique wonders of Yellowstone. His images of the wonders of the area were a significant factor in Congress's decision to establish Yellowstone as our first national park in 1872.

THE AMERICAN CHARACTER

Ralph Waldo Emerson once said, "The true test of a civilization is not the census, nor the size of cities, nor the crops—no, but the kind of man the country turns out."

951 Courage, and the willingness to fight injustice

952 Generosity

953 Warmth and hospitality to strangers

954 Openness of hearts and minds

955 The ability to laugh at life and at ourselves

956 A healthy respect for traditions

957 Strong values

958 A belief in simplicity

959 A healthy disrespect for authority

960 An overriding belief in something greater

961 Willingness to serve the nation in a patriotic way

962 A fundamental belief in free enterprise

963 A powerful and pervasive sense of optimism

964 Self-reliance

965 A willingness to sacrifice

966 Enthusiasm

967 Common sense and practicality

968 A thirst for knowledge and self-improvement

969 Cheering for the underdog

970 A strong sense of community

971 Individualism

972 A constant readiness to set out for new adventures

"Character is like a tree and reputation like its shadow. The shadow is what we think of it; the tree is the real thing."

Abraham Lincoln

"What lies behind us and what lies before us are small matters compared to what lies within us."

Ralph Waldo Emerson

973 The love of freedom

974 The importance of religion in daily life

975 Choosing kindness over cruelty

976 An understanding that every right carries with it a matching responsibility

977 Trustworthiness

978 Fairness

979 Action over words

980 The value of personal initiative

981 A belief in the goodness and reward of hard work

982 An ongoing pioneer spirit

983 A belief in the possible, and sometimes the impossible

AMERICAN HEROES

Many American heroes have demonstrated their patriotism and love of freedom through their heroic efforts and acts of great courage. There are also everyday heroes, ordinary Americans who give of their time and love in order to change the world and to demonstrate that one person can make a difference.

984
Our courageous veterans

985
The men and women who serve in our armed forces

986
All the brave men and
women who have made
the ultimate sacrifice in
the name of freedom

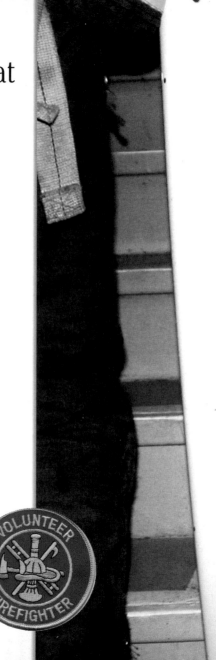

987
Those who stand up for what they believe is right

Mary Harris "Mother" Jones (1837-1930)
An Irish immigrant who worked for more than 50 years as a labor organizer, she was so successful that mine owners called her "the most dangerous woman in America."

Elizabeth Cady Stanton, Susan B. Anthony, Bella Abzug, Gloria Steinem, and all those who stood up and fought for equal rights for women

Margaret Chase Smith (1897-1995)
A Republican senator from Maine from 1949 to 1973, she was one of the first to speak out against Senator Joseph McCarthy. In 1950, along with six other Republican senators, she signed a "Declaration of Conscience" against McCarthy, who falsely accused U.S. citizens of being communists and alleged communist infiltration in the government and show business.

988
Our firefighters, police officers and emergency workers: heroes who risk their lives each day to save and protect us all

Firefighter Mike Kehoe of Engine 28 enters Tower One of the World Trade Center on the morning of September 11, 2001 to assist in the evacuation effort. He escaped before the building collapsed.

Rosa Parks

All those who gave of themselves for the cause of freedom and equal rights

Harriet Tubman and the Underground Railroad

A network of courageous people who helped slaves escape to freedom in the first half of the 1800s.

Rosa Parks (1913-)

On December 1, 1955, Rosa Parks, an African-American woman, boarded a bus in Montgomery, Alabama. When she refused to give up her seat to a white man, she was arrested. Her simple act of defiance led to a 381-day bus boycott and a Supreme Court ruling against segregation on public transportation. Her quiet dignity is inspiring, and shows us that one person can change the world.

Ruby Bridges (1954-)

On November 14, 1960, at the age of 6, Ruby Bridges, escorted by four federal marshalls, walked into William Frantz Elementary School in New Orleans, after a federal court ordered public schools to desegregate. She faced an empty classroom, because white parents kept their children at home. She spent her first year there all alone with the only white teacher who was willing to teach a black child.

The Human Spirit is the thing, after all…
Lewis Hine

990
Lewis Hine

Stating that he "wanted to show things that had to be corrected," Hine pioneered the field of documentary photography as he crossed the country between 1908 and 1924, working for the National Child Labor Committee, recording the exploitation of women and children by industry. His work helped to bring about child protection laws.

Little Brothers-Friends
of the Elderly

991
Little Brothers-Friends of the Elderly

This volunteer-based, non-profit organization is committed to relieving loneliness and isolation among the elderly through friendship, companionship, and socialization opportunities for elders growing old alone. Volunteers give over 53,000 hours of service a year to visit, host parties, deliver emergency food, provide transportation, and take the elderly on outings and vacations.

992
Habitat for Humanity, the ASPCA and the Humane Society, the Make-A-Wish Foundation, America's Second Harvest, the Humane Farming Association, the American Cancer Society, St. Jude Children's Research Hospital, and all the volunteers and donors who give of their time and resources to make our world a better place

993
Those who volunteer to give their time, resources, and love to help others

994
Farm Aid

Started in 1985 by Willie Nelson, John Mellencamp, and Neil Young, Farm Aid concerts have helped keep family farmers on their land.

995
Bob Hope

He made America laugh on radio, television, and in the movies. From his first radio appearance in the 1930s, America loved his quick wit, dry delivery, vaudevillian double takes, and ad libs.

He partnered with Bing Crosby to give us the classic *Road* films of the 1940s and enjoyed a lifelong friendship with Bing both on and off the golf course. Hope hosted the Oscars and played golf with presidents. But Bob Hope's love of his country is best reflected in his USO shows.

Every year from 1942 to 1990, he took his variety show on the road to entertain troops and lift the spirits of GIs stationed all over the world. Over the course of 48 years he brought comedy skits, celebrity appearances, singers, dancers, and gorgeous girls to the South Pacific, Europe, Vietnam, Asia, and the Middle East. Hope wanted to give the troops a reminder "of what they were fighting for," a reminder of home and American life. From 1973 to 1982, Hope entertained at military and veterans' hospitals.

Bob Hope was made an honorary veteran by an act of Congress, signed by President Bill Clinton, in 1997. Expressing his deep feelings about the award, Hope said, "I've been given many awards in my lifetime, but to be numbered among the men and women I admire most is the greatest honor I have ever received." In May 2003, Bob Hope celebrated his 100th birthday with the comment, "I'm so old they've cancelled my blood type." He passed away in July 2003. Thanks for the memories.

Those who carry with them our dream that the little guy can someday win the race

It wasn't just greatness

In 1938, near the end of a decade of monumental turmoil, the year's number one newsmaker was not Franklin Delano Roosevelt, Hitler, or Mussolini. It wasn't Pope Pius XI, nor was it Lou Gehrig, Howard Hughes, or Clark Gable. The subject of the most newspaper column inches in 1938 wasn't even a person. It was an undersized, crooked-legged racehorse named Seabiscuit.

. . . They had come from nowhere. The horse, a smallish, mud-colored animal with forelegs that didn't straighten all the way . . . His jockey, Red Pollard, was a tragic-faced young man who had been abandoned as a boy at a makeshift racetrack cut through a Montana hay field . . . Seabiscuit's trainer, a mysterious, virtually mute mustang breaker named Tom Smith, was a refugee from the vanishing frontier, bearing with him generations of lost wisdom about the secrets of horses . . . Seabiscuit's owner, a broad, beaming former cavalryman named Charles Howard, had begun his career as a bicycle mechanic before parlaying 21 cents into an automotive empire.

. . . Along the way, the little horse and the men who rehabilitated him captured the American imagination. It wasn't just greatness that drew the people to them. It was their story.

Laura Hillenbrand
Seabiscuit, An American Legend

Seabiscuit, the legendary racehorse, who beat the great War Admiral and inspired the nation during the Great Depression.

997
The 1980 Olympic Hockey Team
U. S. Olympic Hockey Came of Age in 1980

It was a miracle. Millions of Americans watched it unfold on TV that night of February 22, 1980. The Cold War was at its peak, and the country was in the doldrums, but the underdog U.S. hockey team, trained by the great coach, Herb Brooks, capitalized on every Russian miscue and used their speed to heat up the action in the rink in Lake Placid, New York.

The Americans played as a team, every man doing his utmost, looking as if they had been together for years. In reality they had been training only a year and a half as a unit. When the final buzzer sounded, the Americans had defeated Russia, and those Americans who had stayed up to see it went a little crazy. The US team went on to beat Finland for the gold medal...a miracle medal.

998

Those who believe in the vision of America's bright future

I HAVE A DREAM that one day this nation will rise up and live out the true meaning of its creed: "We hold these truths to be self-evident: that all men are created equal." I have a dream that one day on the red hills of Georgia the sons of former slaves and the sons of former slaveowners will be able to sit down together at a table of brotherhood. I have a dream that one day even the state of Mississippi, a desert state, sweltering with the heat of injustice and oppression, will be transformed into an oasis of freedom and justice. I have a dream that my four children will one day live in a nation where they will not be judged by the color of their skin but by the content of their character. I have a dream today.

from Martin Luther King Jr.'s speech, delivered on the steps of the Lincoln Memorial in Washington, DC, on August 28, 1963

Martin Luther King Jr.
The father of the civil rights movement in America, Dr. King participated in the Montgomery, Alabama, bus boycott and organized the March on Washington involving 200,000 people. For his commitment to change through non-violent protest, he was awarded the Nobel Peace Prize in 1964.

Immigrants
arriving at
Ellis Island

999
The dream of becoming an American citizen

A Russian family of
27 arriving in New York
September 16, 1921

1000
In America, anything is possible.

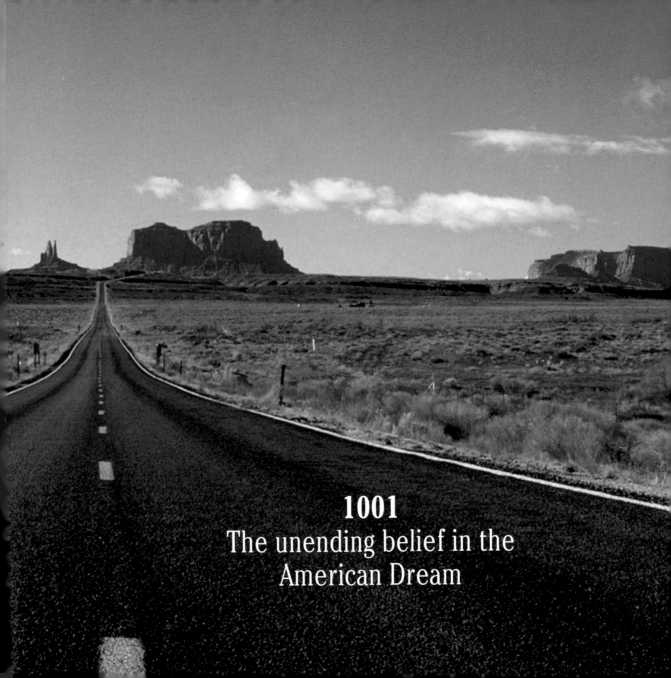

1001
The unending belief in the
American Dream

A Few More Reasons to Love America

Doggie bags
Superman
Austin Powers
Flash Gordon
Luke Skywalker
Pez
Ferris Bueller's Day Off
Buying poppys to help the veterans
Air Jordans
The Love Boat
FUBU
Jennifer Lopez
Daydream Believer by the Monkees
Driving along Lake Shore Drive
The Museum of Modern Art
The enormous Sunday *New York Times*
Sports Bars
Free popcorn at sports bars
Buffalo herds
Sunrise over Iowa
Spring break
Studio 54
Super hero lunch boxes
Frango Mints from Marshall Fields
Cannery Row
The Stairmaster
Richard Simmons
The 1939 New York World's Fair
Saturday Night Live
Pontoon boats
Swap meets
The Saturday Evening Post
Life Magazine
Ben & Jerry's Cherry Garcia Ice Cream
Knee high by the fourth of July
Skelly truck stops

Interstate 80
Charlevoix, Michigan
Sleeping Bear Dunes
Dune buggies
The Magic Eight Ball
The Amazing Kreskin
Red Skelton
Jack Benny
Jackie Gleason
The Rat Pack
The fountain at the Bellagio Hotel in
    Las Vegas
Canoe trips in the Boundary Waters
White Keds
Polio vaccine
Jonas Salk
Harvard, Yale and Princeton
Reading for the Blind
Biscuits and gravy
Singing along to classic rock on
    a car trip
The Circle Line
Winter mornings in the Hamptons
Collecting shells on Sanibel Island
New Hope, Pennsylvania
Big Two-Hearted River
Laughing Whitefish Falls
Aksarben
The Quad Cities
The Twin Cities
The Four Corners
Navaho flat bread
Harry Caray: "Holy Cow!"
Furby
America Online
Frank Lloyd Wright

Taking a tour of the Crayola Crayons
    factory in Easton, Pennsylvania
Coon Rapids, Iowa: Home of the
    World's Largest Corn Cob Pile
Starbucks
Wendy's
Jiffy Lube
The Pep Boys
Long-neck beers
The NBA
NASCAR
Big Ten football competitions
Plymouth Rock
Seventeen Magazine
TV Guide
Vanity Fair
Break dancing
Vinyl siding
Bob Vila
This Old House
Hard Rock Café
Skateboarders
Popular Mechanics
Oprah Winfrey
The theme song from *Gilligan's Island*
Dobie Gillis
The Library of Congress
Bob Dylan
Mr. Tambourine Man
Dave Matthews
John Updike
John Irving
The World According to Garp
Steve McQueen
The Supreme Court
Dr. Henry Kissinger

All in the Family
Mork and Mindy
Three's Company
Howdy Doody
Dots, Raisinettes and Milk Duds
Lollapalooza
Renaissance Festivals
Six Flags Over Texas
Great Adventure
Bugs Bunny, Daffy Duck and Tweety Bird
The Harlem Globetrotters
Sweet Georgia Brown
Popeye and Olive Oyl
Farfel
Shari Lewis and Lambchop
iPods, iMacs, iTunes
Imus in the Morning
Yankees vs. Red Sox
Rah Rah for Old Notre Dame
Anthony Robbins
Paul Harvey, Good Day!
NYPD
Westminster Kennel Club Dog Show
The Houston Astrodome
Yankee Stadium
Who Shot J.R.?
Saturday Night Live
Saturday Night Fever
The Coneheads
Pat Conroy's *Prince of Tides*
The Great Gatsby
Lewis and Clark
Pocahontas
Longfellow
Crazy Horse
Black Elk Speaks

Sitting Bull
Geronimo
Tina Turner
Tippecanoe and Tyler Too
The Alamo
The Baby Boom
Bazooka Joe
Prairie dogs
Earth Day
Paul Revere
Ulysses S. Grant
Donald Trump
Bill Gates
Sam Walton
Navajo, Hopi, Sioux, Cherokee tribes
The Nut Museum, Old Lyme,
    Connecticut
The Chia Pet
The Clapper
George Foreman's Lean Mean
    Fat-Reducing Grilling Machine
Aerosmith
Iron Butterfly
In-A-Gadda-Da-Vida, 1968
The Grateful Dead
Traffic
American Pie
The Jefferson Airplane
Wall Drugs, South Dakota
South of the Border, Dillon,
    South Carolina
Burger Joints
Zingerman's Deli, Ann Arbor, Michigan
El Charro Café, Tucson, Arizona
Pinnacle Peak Patio, Carefree, Arizona
Corky's, Memphis, Tennessee
Bon Ton Café, New Orleans, Louisiana
The Hamburger Hall of Fame,
    Seymour, Wisconsin

The Liberace Museum, Las Vegas
The Museum of Dirt, Boston
The National Cowgirl Museum & Hall of
    Fame, Fort Worth, Texas
The National Cowboy Hall of Fame,
    Oklahoma City
Tiger Stadium, Detroit
The Sunset Strip
Hollywood and Vine
Rodeo Drive
State Street, that great street
Helen Keller
The Americans with Disabilities Act
The Freedom of Information Act
The Round Table at the Algonquin
Take Our Daughters to Work Day
Margaret Mead
Snoopy, Lucy, Linus and Charlie Brown
Flapjacks
Elvis impersonators
Secretariat, Seattle Slew, Man O' War,
    War Admiral, Native Dancer and
    Smarty Jones
Texas toast
The St. Paul Winter Carnival
The Mermaid Parade, Coney Island
Alcoholics Anonymous
Man Ray
Bye Bye Birdie
Raymond Chandler novels
*Midnight in the Garden of
    Good and Evil*
Mary Kay Cosmetics
Erma Bombeck's warm and humorous
    views of American family life
Dear Abby and Ann Landers
The angular Dick Tracy
Mr. Potato Head
Schwinn bicycles

Lincoln Logs
Tinker Toys
Gary Larson
Rin Tin Tin
Hula
Canyon Ranch
The Peace Corps
Down by the Old Mill Stream
Moonlight Bay
Shine On, Harvest Moon
Clementine
A Streetcar Named Desire
Inherit the Wind
A Raisin in the Sun
Death of a Salesman
Born Yesterday
Our Town
The Wabash Cannonball
Rails to Trails Conservancy
Wyatt Earp
Patrick Henry
Robert Ballard
RAGBRAI: The Des Moines Register's
    Annual Great Bicycle Ride Across Iowa
The Blue Hole of Castalia, Ohio
Burma Shave signs
Nancy Lopez
Mia Hamm
Greg Louganis
The North American International Auto
    Show, Detroit, Michigan
The Rock and Roll Hall of Fame and
    Museum, Cleveland
The pageantry and hoopla of the
    Democratic and Republican National
    Conventions, filled with impassioned
    speeches, bouncing signs, strange
    hats and a million balloons
The American Folk Art Museum

The lighthouses of Maine
Dave Barry's newspaper columns
Doonesbury
Archie, Veronica and Jughead
Little Orphan Annie
Zoot suits
Turtle races
Soap box derbies
Potato sack races
State fair pie eating contests
Wide open spaces

And most of all,
the American
people whose
love of freedom
and optimism
 make this country
a symbol of hope
and possibilities.

Acknowledgments

We would like arrange a ticker tape parade to thank our publisher, Leslie Stoker, our wonderful editor, Anne Kostick, the ever patient Kim Tyner, and everyone at STC who believed in us throughout this large endeavor. A Fourth of July fireworks display would be an appropriate gesture of gratitude for our contributing writers, editors, and photographers Tricia Irish, William Polk, Milbry Polk, Sue and Bernie Smith, Bruce Johnson, and Robin Siegel for their wonderful work, creativity, knowledge, humor, patience, and interest. A Congressional Medal of Honor should go to Saundra Sheffer, Carol Elevitch, Diana Lee, and the amazing Angela Escalante, who kept us on track and organized from beginning to end. And to all our wonderful friends and family who shared their ideas and encouragement, we thank you.

⧟

Text credits: page 88, 164 Extracts from *Dateline America*, by Charles Kuralt, Copyright ©1979, published by Harcourt Brace Jovanovich, Inc., New York; page 92, from *Sounds of Spring*, by Ron Green, 1973; page 175, from *Route 66, The Mother Road*, by Michael Wallis, Copyright ©1990, published by St. Martin's Press LLC, New York; page 180, from *The American Language*, by H. L. Mencken, Copyright ©1937, published by Alfred A. Knopf, Inc., New York; page 235, from *Boogie Woogie* by William Russell, from *Jazzmen*, Frederic Ramsey, Jr. and Charles Edward Smith, Copyright ©1939, published by Harcourt Brace Jovanovich, Inc., New York; page 243, from *From Flappers 2 Rappers, American Youth Slang*, by Tom Dalzell, Copyright ©1996, published by Merriam-Webster, Incorporated, Massachusetts.

Image credits: Pages 10, 62, 81, 145,148, 187, 246, 257, ©2004 Tricia Irish Photography; pages 4, 6, 16, 19, 24, 30, 33, 38, 40, 41, 42, 43, 45, 47, 48, 52, 53, 107, 110, 114, 134, 158, 159, 162, 163, 166, 178, 180, 224, 252, 253, 256, 261, 274, 276, 284, 285, 287, 300, 301, 312, 313 courtesy of The Library of Congress; page 27 courtesy of the LBJ Presidential Library; pages 2, 5, 7, 8, 14, 18, 22, 29, 31, 32, 34, 35, 37, 49, 51, 55, 57, 58, 59, 60, 61, 63, 64, 66, 67, 69, 70, 71, 72, 73, 74, 75, 76, 77, 78, 79, 80, 87, 88, 89, 90, 91, 92, 93, 94, 95, 96, 97, 99, 102, 103, 106, 112, 116. 118, 119, 121, 124, 126, 127, 130, 146, 147, 149, 150, 154, 156, 160, 161, 162, 163, 164, 167, 168, 169, 170, 171, 172, 175, 176, 177, 182, 184, 185, 187, 188, 190, 191, 192, 194, 195, 197, 198, 199, 200, 206, 207, 208, 209, 213, 214, 215, 216, 217, 219, 220, 221, 222, 223, 226, 227, 240, 241, 243, 248, 249, 250, 251, 254, 256, 258, 259, 275, 288, 289, 290, 293, 294, 296, 312, 316 from the Tiegreen Collection; pages 64, 65 courtesy of Sydney's Roadside Cafe, Nyack, NY; page 84, Courtesy of Steak 'N Shake, Inc.; page 86, Courtesy of Anne Kerman; page 16 courtesy of Anne Kostick; page 108 courtesy of SturgisMainStreetPhoto.com, South Dakota (photographer MissBHavin.com); pages 149, 152 courtesy of Susan Goodman Smith; page 194 courtesy of The World's Largest Catsup Bottle, Collinsville, IL; page 195 courtesy of the Corn Palace, Mitchell, SD, (photographer Rich Stedman); page 79, courtesy of Michael Stefanos, Chicago, IL; page 160 courtesy of the National Park Services; page 203 courtesy of Crayola Crayons, Binney & Smith Inc., Easton, PA; page 229 photograph © Skip Bolen; page 262, 265, 266, 267, 268, 270 courtesy of U.S. Air Force; page 264, 269 courtesy of U.S. Navy; page 271, 272, 273 courtesy of NASA; page 302 courtesy of Little Brothers-Friends of the Elderly, Chicago, IL; page 13, 17, 36, 46, 68, 100, 104,105, 109, 115, 120, 122. 123, 125, 128, 131, 132, 133, 137, 138, 141, 143, 151, 196, 202, 205, 207, 211, 212, 230, 232, 234, 237, 238, 241, 242, 245, 278, 279, 281, 283, 297, 298, 303, 304, 307, 309, 311, 314 AP/Wide World Photos; page 19, 20 courtesy of National Archives; page 54, 82, 193 ©2004 Michael Witzel/Coolstock.com; pages 174, 189 ©2004 Howard Ande/Coolstock.com; page 186 ©2004 Ron Saari/Coolstock.com; 168, 169 courtesy of America's Byways.org.